A Short History
of the
Interpretation
of the Bible

St. Michael's Episcopal Church
Little Rock, Arkansas

A Short History
of the
Interpretation
of the Bible

Second Edition
Revised and Enlarged

ROBERT GRANT

with
DAVID TRACY

FORTRESS PRESS   PHILADELPHIA

Library of Congress Cataloging in Publication Data

Grant, Robert McQueen, 1917–
  A short history of the interpretation of the Bible.

  Bibliography: p.
  Includes indexes.
  1. Bible—Criticism, interpretation, etc.—History.
I. Tracy, David. II. Title.
BS500.G7 1984   220.6′09   83–18485
ISBN 0–8006–1762–2 (pbk.)

K469H83   Printed in the United States of America 1–1762

Contents

PART 2 BY DAVID TRACY

Preface
to the First Edition

Fifteen years ago, when this book appeared as *The Bible in the Church*, American concern for the history of interpretation was not so widespread as it has come to be since then. Perhaps for this reason, among others, it now seems advisable to make some changes as the book goes forth again. The basic historical information remains much the same. My own views, influenced by further study, chiefly of the New Testament and of the early church, have been modified; and I have tried at several points to set them forth more systematically. The principal changes, therefore, occur at the beginning and the end of the book. At the end I have decided to refrain from prophecy, and, instead, to set forth what I regard as the basic principles of historical and theological interpretation. The quotations from the Greek New Testament are in my own translation.

It would be impossible to express my thanks to everyone who by criticism, debate, or discussion has helped me to move a little toward clarity; it would be equally impossible not to mention my colleagues and students in the Divinity School of the University of Chicago.

1963   R.M.G.

Preface
to the Second Edition

The first edition appeared twenty-one years ago. Meanwhile theologians and philosophers have been exceedingly active in this area, and I am fortunate indeed to have taken David Tracy aboard as our pilot. He brings the whole book into its new port. Meanwhile I have made a few changes mostly in the first six chapters, partly out of further reading, partly for the sake of clarity. Both of us believe that the book holds together and has something rather straightforwardly theological (and historical) to contribute.

1984   Robert M. Grant

PART 1

1

Introduction

The story of the Bible in the church is a long and complex one. In the course of Christian history many methods have been employed in order to interpret the record of God's revelation. For the interpretation of scripture is the principal bond between the ongoing life and thought of the church and the documents which contain its earliest traditions. In past ages it has often been thought necessary to justify every doctrine of the church by explicit or implicit statements of scripture. And yet the scriptures are usually addressed to specific occasions to meet specific needs. The universal and permanent meaning of many passages of scripture does not seem to have been intended by its authors. On the other hand, when scripture is regarded as completely sufficient for doctrine, and at the same time the needs of the contemporary situation are quite different from needs long past, some means has to be found for relating the ancient book to the thought and life of a later day. This task is performed by interpretation.

It has been suggested that the more similar the situation of a later individual or group is to the situation of Bible times, the simpler will be the interpreter's task. Such a suggestion does less than justice to the diversity present among those who in various circumstances recorded their own responses, and their communities' responses, to the revelation of God. Environmental situations have influenced prophets, evangelists, and interpreters. But in spite of the varying environments and the diversity of responses—to which the author of Hebrews points in his opening period—there is a unity which is based on a fundamental presupposition: God lives and works in history; he has chosen a people to be his own; he has guided, and still guides, the course of this people's life and work, in spite of its rebellion against him. Without acknowledgment of this presupposition, at least as a working hypothesis, biblical interpretation is impossible. When Gnostics insisted that the real God was quite different from, and even opposed to, the God of the Old Testament, they could hardly understand the revelation of the God whom Jesus called Father. When Alexandrian theologians laid tremendous emphasis upon the impassibility of God, they had to allegorize away the passages, in Old and New Testament alike, in which it is quite clear that God is not impassible. A faulty theology used a faulty method of exegesis as its instrument.

Our study will examine the principal methods which Christians have employed in the interpretation of scripture, and the circumstances which led to their employment. We shall also show briefly through what channels these methods came into existence, and through what channels they came into the church. Sometimes methods were taken over unchanged from other sources by Christians; sometimes methods were taken over and altered; sometimes almost entirely new methods were devised. We shall lay special emphasis on the early and formative period of the church's life, for in it were sown the seeds of almost every later development, and later interpreters have often claimed that they were returning to the methods of the early church. Our investigations will not attempt to cover every period of the church's history, but only those times in which significantly new developments took place in regard to the interpretation of scripture. Some more detailed and more inclusive works will be found listed in the select bibliography.

Our study is in part a historical sketch of *hermeneutics*, the methodology of interpretation. But since this word seems to have been lost in ordinary English usage, we have employed interpretation, a much broader term, in its place. The interpretation of any written record of human thought is the exposition of its author's meaning in terms of our own thought forms. Though we may try to think his thought after him, ultimately our own mind must determine the way in which we express his meaning. Interpretation is always subjective as well as objective.

A distinction is sometimes made between interpretation and *exegesis*. On this view interpretation is the task of the theologian, while exegesis is for the biblical specialist who explains both theological and nontheological materials and offers his work for the use of theology. In our study we tend to reject this distinction and use the two terms as equivalent. The reason for this fusion will become evident in the course of the book, especially in the discussion of the Reformation.

A new problem for exegesis has arisen in modern times. Many ancient Christians claimed that the scriptures had been given by God to his church, just as in rabbinic thought the Torah was the peculiar possession of Israel. Others might read, but they could never understand. To Paul, for example, the interpretation of scripture was possible only through a charismatic gift of the Holy Spirit. Later Christian writers developed more fully the theory of the Bible as the church's book. Only those who stood in the succession from Christ (as among the rabbis those who stood in the succession from Moses) could interpret the sacred book. Outsiders—with the exception of such writers as "Longinus"—examined scripture only in order to attack its defenders. With the Renaissance and the revival and diffusion of learning, this situation changed. Lorenzo Valla critically investigated scripture as well as the *Donation of Constantine*; John Colet turned from his study of Greek literature to examine the epistle to the Romans. Philosophers like Hobbes and Spinoza prepared the way for eighteenth-century deism. The Reformation was not alone responsible for the modern study of the Bible, although certainly it increased men's interest in questions of the meaning of scripture. In nineteenth-century Germany the critical movement reached its peak. The attempt was made to understand the Bible historically, at the same time that the rise of classical philology made possible the historical understanding of other ancient books. This historical method still lives, and presents a constant problem to those who wish to build a modern theology on the foundation of biblical criticism. By its most ardent defenders its methods are set forth with a rigidity unequalled by scholastic theologians, and its excesses have aroused suspicion not only among simple believers but among skeptical theologians as well.

Yet in our time the historical understanding of any ancient text is inevitable, and it is not possible for us to turn our backs on past centuries of historical investigation. Today it is our task to reexamine the methods of biblical interpretation and to test them anew. It is often maintained that the historical method is the only means which can be employed in interpreting the Bible. On the other hand, it is held that the historical method leads to antiquarianism or 'historicism.' In my opinion, as will be seen in the last chapter of this book, both these views are correct. It is impossible for modern people to avoid thinking historically, but their understanding of what historical thinking involves is often inadequate. It does not mean that we should try to think in a B.C.E. manner when we deal with the Old Testament, or that in dealing with the gospels we should pretend that we live before the church came into being. Instead, a truly historical method requires us to take *all* the historical evidence into account, and this evidence includes the purposes for which our documents were written, preserved, and transmitted. In addition, the study of the documents requires what Wilhelm Dilthey called "inner affinity and sympathy."[1] We enter into a conversation with the documents and the authors who stand behind them; we do not simply judge them.

It remains true that the proper place for the Bible is in the church. The church existed before the creation of scripture; it is the environment of scripture. Both church and scripture witness to Christ; but the church came first, and scripture was produced within the church for the use of the members of the body. This environment often allows a sympathetic understanding of scripture, an insight into its genius.

Yet unless investigators into the problems of scripture can remain free; unless they can examine questions of interpretation without being unduly influenced by dogmatic considerations; unless, in short, they are not only church people but also free scholars, how can they hope to understand the Bible and make its insights available for their contemporaries? In a divided age such as ours, such a question can find its answer more readily than in the past. It is a problem of tensions. Such tensions between two authorities, each with its own claim upon the loyalty of the interpreters, are more fruitful than simple resolutions of difficulties. Interpreters are not only responsible to the truth as they see it (and the truth can never be as others would like to have them see it) but also to the Christian community, within whose succession of worshippers they stand and to which they are responsible. Humans are not only rational animals but also worshipping ones. And there must always be a tension between the mystery which they worship and the truth about the mystery which they attempt to understand.

Interpreters of scripture have also to realize that like all Christians they stand not only in the community which is the church but also in the community which is the world outside. Much of the story which they read in the Bible is the story of the smaller group, told from the inside by one within; but there is also an outside history, and the two overlap. If they concentrate solely on the inner story, their understanding will be mythological, irrational, pietistic; if they know nothing but the story of the world outside, their myth will disappear in matter-of-factness, their sense of God's working in the world will be lost, and they will produce "scientific history." Both elements together, however, will set the church in the village and the village in the world. Both elements together make possible an apologetic or constructive theology. Both elements together are needed to portray the mystery of one who became flesh.

2

Jesus and
the Old Testament

Naturally enough, the interpretation of the Bible in Christianity begins with Jesus. This fact might seem sufficiently obvious not to
require notice, were it not for the tendency of many modern historical critics to assume that Jesus must have conformed completely
to what they call 'normative' Judaism. Therefore, they go on to
conclude, he must have interpreted the Old Testament, the Bible
of Judaism, just as any other Jewish exegete of his day would have
expounded it. There is no novelty in his message, at least insofar
as it is an interpretation of the Old Testament. And since a great
deal of his message is built upon the foundations of Old Testament
theology, there can hardly be any novelty in the methods of interpretation which he employed.

Yet there is a saying in the tractate Sanhedrin of the Babylonian
Talmud which ought to give these critics pause. "He who says,
'The Torah is not from God,' or even if he says 'The whole Torah
is from God with the exception of this or that verse which not God
but Moses spoke from his own mouth'—that soul shall be rooted
up."[1] Jewish exegetes believed that every word of scripture had
been spoken by God. There could be no question of its inspiration
or authenticity. And anyone who uttered such a question clearly
revealed his own separateness from the holy congregation of Israel. Jesus, on the other hand, finds a distinct difference between
the words by which God joined together Adam and Eve in an en-
during bond of marriage and the words by which Moses tempo-
rized with the people's hardheartedness and permitted divorce
(Mark 10:2ff.). Moses spoke for a special situation and neglected
the purpose of God at Creation.

Clearly Jesus, while he is a Jew and while his mission is primarily to his own people and is expressed in the terms of their

8

thought, does not hesitate to distinguish between parts of scripture in which God is more or less fully revealed. It is this discrimination which underlies all later Christian developments of the theory of interpretation. And yet we must not overemphasize the difference between Jesus and his contemporaries. There are significant resemblances as well.

To Jesus, as to other first-century Jews, the scriptures were authoritative and inspired. To his opponents, whether human or superhuman, he can quote scripture and say, "It is written . . ." (Mark 11:17; Matt. 4:4; Luke 4:4, and so on). He can ask them, "Have you not read . . . ?" (Mark 2:25). And he can stress the divine source of inspiration of scripture by saying, "David himself said in the Holy Spirit" (Mark 12:36). This is an especially interesting passage, for we find in the contemporary writings of Philo of Alexandria the concept of the inspired writer as an instrument of God. The Holy Spirit of God uses him as a flute and breathes through him. Jesus' expression is not so mechanical. It is the Holy Spirit which inspires David; but it is David who speaks. This is the same emphasis on the human side of inspiration which we find in Jesus' discussion of Moses' bill of divorcement.

Like his contemporaries, Jesus regards Moses as the author of the Pentateuch and David as the author of the Psalms. He was not a literary or historical critic; indeed, it would be incredible if the tradition had reported any interest on his part in literary questions. He regards the events of the Old Testament times as real events. God made male and female (Mark 10:6); Abel was murdered (Matt. 23:35; Luke 11:51); and so on. And yet they are more than historical events. They have direct relevance to the times in which Jesus stands. When David was hungry he ate the shewbread; the regulations of cult must be subordinated to human needs; the Sabbath was made for man (Mark 2:25ff.). With such an appeal to the religious content of scripture as against its merely literal or legal form, Jesus sweeps away the accumulated dust of tradition; he teaches "as one with authority, and not as the scribes" (Mark 1:22). And we are therefore not surprised when he attacks the authoritative exegetes of his day with the ironic statement: "You do well to set aside the commandment of God in order to keep your tradition" (Mark 7:9).

In Jesus' view of scripture there was a strong emphasis on moral command and personal relations as contrasted with merely cultic prescriptions. His attitude toward the Sabbath and the legal requirement of ritual cleanliness (Mark 7:1ff.) illustrates this emphasis. He quoted definite passages of scripture to support his point of view. In Hos. 6:6 he finds the expression, "I desire mercy and not sacrifice" (Matt. 9:13; 12:7). Or again, in Isa. 29:13 he finds his opponents described: "This people honors me with their lips, but their heart is far from me; in vain they worship me, teaching as doctrine the ordinances of men" (Mark 6:6f.). Finally, he finds the present state of the temple foretold in Isa. 56:7 and Jer. 7:2: "My house shall be called a house of prayer of all nations; but you have made it a den of thieves" (Mark 11:17). The prophetic reinterpretation of religion is close to that of Jesus himself. And when he comes to express in a single sentence the key to the meaning of the whole law of the Old Testament, he makes use of a passage from Deuteronomy, the Shema, which every Israelite recited daily: "Hear, Israel, the Lord our God is one Lord, and thou shalt love the Lord thy God . . ." (Mark 9:29f.). With this passage he joins the other "law of love" from the Holiness Code of Leviticus: "Thou shalt love thy neighbor as thyself" (Mark 12:31). Jesus' statement is clear and explicit: "There is no other commandment greater than these." The evangelist Matthew reinterprets it only slightly when he says, "On these two commandments hang all the Law and the prophets" (Matt. 22:40).

The systematic arrangement of the Sermon on the Mount doubtless owes much to the evangelist Matthew.[2] Perhaps the series of antitheses beginning "You have heard . . . but I say," is not so closely knit as Matthew would have us believe; but as a whole the passage (Matt. 5:21–48) reproduces accurately the attitude of Jesus toward the legal portions of the Old Testament. He is a highly independent teacher. He might accurately be called a nonconformist. He does not set aside the Law, however; he deepens it, reinforces it, raises it all to its highest moral level. It is sometimes said that the expression, "You have heard . . . but I say," is characteristic of Jewish exegesis; but the examples adduced are not very convincing.[3] The expression is far more characteristic of Jesus himself, whose teaching is a teaching with personal authority. His exegesis is more unlike than like that of his contemporaries.

We have not yet mentioned the way in which Jesus' interpretation of the Old Testament is most strikingly individual. Jesus not only proclaims the imminent and somehow already present reign of God; he proclaims the fact that it is the fulfillment of the predictions of the great prophets. "The time is completed and the reign of God has drawn near" (Mark 1:15). This knowledge is not esoteric. It is not a mystery known only to Jesus and his disciples. "How do the scribes say that Elijah must come first? Elijah does come first and renews all things. And how is it written of the Son of Man, that he suffers many things and is set at nought?" (Mark 9:11f.). Here Jesus points out that the Elijah who was to precede the reign of God according to the scribes, is known to him and to them. But what the scribes cannot understand is a figure who suffers. They cannot believe that Isaiah 53 can refer to an individual as well as to the nation. Indeed, Jewish exegesis of Isaiah 53 never interpreted messianically the passages referring to suffering and rejection.[4] Here Jesus' interpretation is unique. He goes beyond contemporary Judaism and interprets the prophecies of the Old Testament in reference to his movement and to himself. It is fairly clear in another passage (Matt. 11:5; Luke 7:22) that Jesus regarded his "signs" as fulfillments of the prophecy of Isaiah. And at the end of his life, in the Last Supper in the upper room, he sealed with his disciples a new covenant which fulfilled the prophecy of Jeremiah (Mark 24:24). To be sure, some of these examples were influenced more by the theological outlook of the early Church than by the remembrance of Jesus, but the idea that he regarded prophecy as somehow fulfilled in himself lies deep in the tradition.

Such an interpretation of scripture was thoroughly repugnant to Jesus' contemporaries. His interpretation of Dan. 7:13 as referring to himself, if we can rely on the rather confused testimony of his investigation by the authorities, was called "blasphemy" by the high priest (Mark 14:64). And his free attitude toward the Law brought the accusation that his mission was its destruction (Matt. 5:17). Yet there are passages, not only in the somewhat Judaistic Gospel of Matthew but also in the Gospel of the gentile Luke, which represent Jesus as upholding a rigorous doctrine of scripture like that held by contemporary rabbis. "All scripture is inspired and helpful for teaching" (2 Tim. 3:16); this is the Jewish doctrine. And it is reflected in Matt. 5:18 (Luke 16:17): "Until heaven and earth pass away, one *yodh*—the smallest letter of the Hebrew alphabet—or one corner of a letter shall not pass away from the Law." Not even one of the least of the commandments can be "loosed" (Matt. 5:19). And in conformity with this doctrine Jesus orders a healed leper to show himself to the priest and make the offering which Moses commanded (Mark 1:44).

This paradoxical attitude of Jesus toward the scriptures is in part due to the way in which his sayings were remembered by conservative groups within Jewish Christianity.[5] But to a greater extent it comes from his own double relation to the Old Testament. The Law in itself is what St. Paul was to call "holy"; the commandment was "holy and righteous and good" (Rom. 7:12). But "love is the fulfillment of the Law" (Rom. 13:10). Moreover the holy history of the Old Testament is significant not only in itself but also in relation to the greater thing which was to come (Matt. 12:38ff.; Luke 11:29ff.). "You have heard that it was said to the ancients"—and for their time it was the word of God to them—"but I say"—I who speak with all the authority of the prophets, and more.

Ancient Christian analysis and more than a century of modern critical study make it impossible for us to employ the Gospel of John in interpreting the thought of Jesus himself. The ideas which we find expressed in this gospel are sometimes derived from genuine tradition of the sayings of Jesus; but they have been transposed into another key by those who handed down the tradition. They do not represent so much what Jesus taught as what the church taught in his name. The Spirit of truth comes later and interprets Jesus to a new generation (John 16:13f.). Nevertheless, the attitude of the Johannine Jesus towards the Old Testament is close to that reported in the synoptic tradition. With his contemporaries in Judaism he knows that Moses gave the Law (John 10:35). And yet Jesus' attitude toward the scriptures is ambiguous. The Law is not all on the same plane. In the Law there is not only the Sabbath but also circumcision; and circumcision takes precedence of the Sabbath (John 7:22). Therefore healings are also permissible on the Sabbath. There is a higher way than legalism. Moreover the Jews search the scriptures because they believe that by them they can attain eternal life. These very scriptures contain an element of prophecy which bears witness to Jesus himself (John 5:39), and this is their true and ultimate meaning. The Jews who do not turn to Jesus are without excuse, for Moses himself has pointed the way. "If you believed Moses, you would believe me; for he wrote concerning me. But if you do not believe his writings, how will you believe my words?" (John 5:46f.). It is the Law without its proper prophetic interpretation to which Jesus refers as "your" Law (John 8:17; 10:34). It is mere law, misunderstood without the Spirit.

In this question of the true meaning of the Law we come close, as we shall see, to the thought of Paul, especially as it is set forth in 2 Corinthians, and it is probable that John was not immune to the insights of his great forerunner to the gentiles. And yet we must avoid mechanical distinctions and oversubtle analyses. Jesus and Paul are not unalike in their attitude towards the question of the Old Testament; and any investigation into the relation of their outlooks which results in sharp antitheses between a Jewish Jesus and a Greek Paul can hardly be correct. Both of them faced the final question of the meaning of the Old Testament for the new Israel of God; and their answers were not dissimilar.

A final question requires our attention. What was the relation of this new understanding of the Old Testament to the exegesis of contemporary rabbis? Let us consider an example in which the form and content of Jesus' interpretation lies close to that of his contemporaries. "You have heard that it was said to the ancients, 'Do not swear falsely, but pay your oaths to the Lord' (Lev. 19:12; Exod. 20:7; Num. 30:2). But I say to you, Do not swear at all; not by heaven, for it is the throne of God; not by earth, for it is the footstool of his feet (Isa. 66:1); not by Jerusalem, for it is the city of the great king (Ps. 48:2); not by your head shall you swear, for you cannot make one hair white or black" (Matt. 5:33ff.). The content of this example of exegesis is Jewish; we may compare Sir. 23:9: "Accustom not thy mouth to an oath, and be not accustomed to the naming of the Holy One." The form is also Jewish; it is what the rabbis called *halakah*, from the verb *halak* (to walk), in the sense of following a way of life.

Another example of Jesus' teaching method which is characteristically Jewish may be found in Mark 12:26f. "Concerning the resurrection of the dead, have you not read in the book of Moses how God spoke to him at the bush and said, 'I am the God of Abraham and the God of Isaac and the God of Jacob' (Exod. 3:6)? He is not the God of the dead but of the living." According to Luke 22:39 some of the scribes said, "Teacher, you have spoken rightly." The answer was typical of the exegesis called *haggada*, theological and mythological interpretation; a very similar example is to be found in 4 Maccabees. It illustrated the statement of the oldest midrash on Deuteronomy: "Those who search out the intimations of scripture say, 'If you wish to know the Creator of the world, learn *haggada*; from it you will come to know God and cleave to his ways.'"[6]

These sayings of Jesus have a strong claim to be regarded as genuine, for while they are thoroughly Jewish in form and content they are preserved in Greek books by Christians to whom the Jewish form was gradually becoming meaningless. And yet they are not simply Jewish. They must be understood in the wider context of all Jesus' sayings. And it must be remembered that there is a striking difference between the underlying eschatological emphasis of Jesus' mission and the rabbis' concentration upon the Law. He looks forward for his inspiration; they look back. Their task has been well described by George Foot Moore in these words:

> To discover, elucidate, and apply what God . . . teaches and enjoins [in the Law] is the task of the scholar as interpreter of scripture. Together with the principle that in God's revelation no word is without significance this conception of scripture leads to an atomistic exegesis, which interprets sentences, clauses, phrases, and even single words, independently of the context or the historical occasion, as divine oracles; combines them with other similarly detached utterances; and makes large use of analogy of expressions, often by purely verbal association.[7]

In form this is sometimes the exegetical method of Jesus, but both he and rabbinic exegetes often transcend it.

In summary we may say that while often the form and some-times the content of the sayings of Jesus is very similar to that of contemporary rabbis, his underlying outlook is somewhat different from theirs. In the first place, he does not hesitate to criticize scripture and to interpret it in relation to its own highest utter-ances, which are words of God. (Hillel did the same.) Love of God and love of neighbor are the two great commandments in whose light the rest must be regarded. In the second place, he fre-quently points to the fulfillment of the prophecies of scripture in his mission. The messianic interpretation of scripture is not novel. We find something closely resembling it in the Dead Sea Scrolls, with their interpretations of prophetic passages as referring to the Teacher of Righteousness. What is novel is Jesus' proclamation that the reign of God is at hand and is being inaugurated in his own work.

Indeed, the story of the paradoxical "triumphal entry" into Jeru-salem seems to show that Jesus was consciously fulfilling the prophecy of Zech. 9:9: "Behold, thy king cometh unto thee, lowly, and riding upon an ass, even upon a colt the foal of an ass." Neither Mark nor Luke refers to the prophecy of the peaceable king; Matthew (21:4) says that the entry took place so that what was spoken through the prophet might be fulfilled; and John (12:16) states that "his disciples did not know these things at first, but when Jesus had been glorified they then remembered that these things had been written of him and that people had done these things for him." Scholars have often suspected that the literary evi-dence shows that the relating of Zechariah to the entry was the cre-ation of the early church. The evidence suggests just as strongly that the relating was the church's discovery of the real intention of Jesus.

At this point there is a difference between ancient and modern understandings of Jesus' mission. An ancient Christian would con-clude that Jesus was simply indicating, in a veiled manner, that he was the king whose coming was predicted by the prophet. Modern students of the gospels might go on to consider the events which, according to Mark and Matthew, follow the entry. They might be impressed by the relation of the cleansing of the temple to the pre-diction of cleansing in Zech. 14:21. They might find the saying about the casting of "this mountain" into the sea (Mark 11:23) related to the prediction of Zech. 14:4 that the Mount of Olives would be split "toward the east and toward the west" (in Hebrew, "toward the sea"). They could then suggest that as Jesus fulfilled one part of the prophecy, either he or his disciples, or both, expected that the rest of the events predicted would take place: since the events did not take place, and the fig tree did not bear fruit out of season, Jesus realized that the cup of suffering was not to be taken away from him (Mark 14:36) and that his way could be only the way of the cross. Such a picture of Jesus' attitude toward prophecy remains conjectural, but it cannot be excluded on dogmatic grounds. For "of that day or that hour no one knows, neither the angels in heaven nor the Son, but only the Father" (Mark 13:32). With ancient theologians, modern students of the gospels have to accept what the New Testament tells them of the humanity of Jesus.

The saying in Matt. 13:52 about the Christian scribe, as Klostermann pointed out,[8] can well be applied to Jesus himself: "Every scribe instructed in the kingdom of heaven is like a householder who brings out of his treasure-chest things new and things old."

3

Paul and
the Old Testament

At the end of the nineteenth century it was customary for critics to distinguish sharply between 'the religion of Jesus' and 'the religion about Jesus.' The first was the highest form of Judaism; the second was Christianity. Sometimes the question was asked, Jesus or Paul?—for Paul was the founder of the Christian faith. More recent study has come to reject this dichotomy, and to insist on the continuity between Jesus and his greatest apostle. This continuity is evident in the attitudes of Jesus and of Paul towards the interpretation of the Old Testament.

Paul was acquainted with collections of sayings of the Lord,[1] and through these he was aware of what Jesus had taught in regard to the Old Testament. The new covenant of the Lord had fulfilled the prophecies of the Old Testament (1 Cor. 11:25). Moreover, the early church before Paul had contributed its own interpretations of the suffering and victory of Christ. His death for our sins and his resurrection on the third day took place "according to the scriptures" (1 Cor. 15:3f.). It is difficult for us to determine how much of his exegetical theory Paul owes to his predecessors in the Christian faith. In any event, the general interpretation of the Old Testament in terms of Christ is due to them.

In the rejection of legalism, Paul's thought resembles the teaching of Jesus. He knows that the Law as a book of legal ordinances was our enemy. It brought a curse even to those who tried to keep its commandments, for in Deut. 27:26 it says, "Cursed is everyone who does not abide in all the things written in the book of the law to do them" (Gal. 3:10). Paul takes the Christian understanding of the Law from Jesus. It is summed up in a single sentence: "Thou shalt love thy neighbor as thyself" (Gal. 5:14; Rom. 13:9).

Both to Jesus and to Paul, the Old Testament is a book of hope.

But Paul, who lives after the death and resurrection of Jesus, is able to discover many messianic allusions which could hardly have been found earlier. For example, his interpretation of Christ as the second Adam is not given him by Jesus himself, but by a combination of current Jewish speculation with Christian awareness of the significance of redemption. The experience of the church, the body of Christ, was also prefigured in the story of Israel. The fathers were "baptized" in the cloud and in the sea at the Exodus, and they ate "spiritual" food and drank "spiritual" drink in the desert. These were foreshadowings of the Eucharist (1 Cor. 10:2ff.).

There are striking differences between the exegetical thought of Jesus and of Paul. Paul lives after the crucifixion. He sees the tragedy of legalism. Christ himself had become "a curse" for us when he was crucified; for the Law says, "Cursed is everyone who hangs on a tree" (Deut. 21:23; Gal. 3:13). While Jesus criticized the Law he did not carry his criticism to the point of absolute rejection. Again, Jesus is not a theologian but the despair of theologians. No systematic treatment can do justice to the richness and variety of his thought. Paul, on the other hand, has a naturally theological mind. His is not our type of theology, to be sure. More often than not, his mind moves allusively, intuitively, by verbal association rather than by any obvious logical process. He was not a Greek, trained in a Platonic or Stoic school, though he probably studied rhetoric; he was a Jew, brought up at Jerusalem at the feet of Gamaliel (Acts 22:3). "Philosophy" for him means only "vain deceit" (Col. 2:8).

There are several passages in his letters where Paul makes some effort to express systematically his conceptions of exegesis. In the first place, we may consider the words which he uses in setting forth the relation between the history contained in the Old Testament and the history of new Israel, the church. The word "type," which he employs several times, ordinarily means simply *example*; in 1 Thess. 1:7 the church at Thessalonica is described as "an example to all the believers in Macedonia and Achaea," while in 2 Thess. 3:9 the apostle himself is an example for them to imitate. In 1 Cor. 10:6 the word is used in what was to become a semitechnical expression. The whole story of the Exodus took place on behalf of us who are Christians; "these things were our types, so that we should not be desirers of evil." In an earlier passage the same thought is expressed without the use of the word. "In the law of Moses it is written: Thou shalt not muzzle the ploughing ox. Does God care for oxen? or does he speak, doubtless, on our account? For us it was written" (1 Cor. 9:9f.). Here the idea is not so much of an obvious example, or type, as of a hidden mystery, which might almost be called allegory.[2] In Rom. 5:14 Adam is called "a type of one to come." He is not simply an example, for he corresponds to Christ not only by resemblance but also by difference. In many instances Christ comes to reverse his work; Paul emphasizes this relationship in 1 Corinthians 15.

Another word lies close to Greek rather than to Jewish exegetical theory, and yet when we examine Paul's use of the expression, we see that it lies within the limits of Judaism. He employs the word in his letter to the Galatians:

It is written, Abraham had two sons, one from the slave girl and one from the free [Gen. 16:15]. The one from the slave girl was born according to the flesh, but the one from the free, through the promise. These things are *meant allegorically*: for they are two covenants, one from Mount Sinai in Arabia; but it is parallel to the present Jerusalem, for it is in slavery with its own children. But the Jerusalem above is free; which is our mother [Gal. 4:22–26].

The word *meant allegorically* (*allegoroumena*) is from a verb commonly used by Greek interpreters, especially by Stoics who interpreted allegorically and explained away the myths concerning the gods. According to these exegetes, some of whom were Paul's contemporaries, "saying one thing and signifying something other than what is said is called allegory."[3] They proceeded to interpret Homer, for example, as if it were an allegory. They looked for hidden mysteries under the outward forms. Similarly Paul goes far beyond the literal or historical understanding of the story in Genesis when he finds in it prefigured the enslaved Israel and the free. He is reading into it a theory which the story cannot literally bear. But his interpretation is not quite the same as allegorization. He does not deny the reality of the Old Testament history. Moreover, there is a sense in which the figures of the Old Testament were actually intended to be examples, and if it is proper to look for such examples in Exodus or Deuteronomy, it is also proper to find them in the story of Abraham's two sons. Paul's theory is not entirely forced.[4]

Our understanding of Paul's interpretation of the Old Testament does not depend merely on the words which he uses in setting it forth. More important is the content which he is able to find in scripture. His exegesis is Christocentric. To him Jesus is the promised Messiah, and not only the passages which explicitly foretell his coming, but the scriptures as a whole, are full of references to him. We have already seen that Paul finds the death and resurrection of Christ pretypified in scripture. He does not say where the types are to be found, but we may suspect that in Isaiah 53 he found the death of Christ, and in Hos. 7:2 (or perhaps in the book of Jonah) he found his resurrection.

For Paul, as for ancient Christians generally, the meaning of Christ was not to be understood apart from the history of God's plan of redemption which, beginning with the old Israel, found its culminating point in the creation of a new Israel, the church. Paul shares with other Christians an understanding of the mystery of God's working in history. This understanding is both based on and largely responsible for his exegesis. In the light of his experience of the crisis of human history which confronted him in Christ, he finds other crises in the history of Israel, and believes that they are types which prefigure the events of his own day. The first crisis is that of Adam's fall, by which sin and death entered the world (Rom. 5:12). The second crisis is the faithfulness of Abraham, which was "reckoned to him for righteousness" (Gal. 3:6). The third crisis is the giving of the Law through angels to Moses, "because of transgressions" (Gal. 3:19). The fourth crisis is the crucifixion and resurrection of Christ. Each of these crises is meaningful for us, for each took place on behalf of us who are Christians. "As in Adam all die, so in Christ all shall be made alive." (1 Cor. 15:22). The promise of blessing which God made to Abraham and to his seed applies to Christ, and therefore to Christians (Gal. 3:16). Christ has redeemed us from the Law (Gal. 3:13); "the law of the Spirit of life in Christ Jesus has freed you from the Law of sin and death" (Rom. 8:2). And the crucifixion and resurrection of Christ point forward to our own death and resurrection with him (Rom. 6:3f.; Col. 3:1ff.).[5]

A significant example of Paul's rabbinic exegesis is to be found in one of the proofs which he gives for his interpretation of the biblical history:

> The promises were spoken to Abraham and to his seed. It does not say, And to seeds, as in the case of many, but, as in the case of one, And to thy seed—who is Christ [Gal. 3:16].

In Gen. 13:15 (17:19) the word "seed" is of course a collective noun. It refers to the heirs of Abraham considered as a whole. By insisting on a rigorous literalism which he elsewhere ignores (2 Cor. 11:22), Paul is able to interpret the word in reference to Christ. How can he do so? He is not considering Christ merely as an individual, but as constituting a body with all the righteous who live by faith in him. The blessing of Abraham does not come down to Christ alone, but to us. It might almost be said that "Christ" is a collective noun as well as "seed." While the form of Paul's exegesis is rabbinic and verbal, its underlying thought is more profound.[6]

Another interesting example is set forth in 1 Corinthians 10:1ff., where the experience of the children of Israel at the Exodus is understood as an example for Christians. In the verse from Galatians cited above, Paul relies on a completely literal and verbal exegesis; in this passage from 1 Corinthians, his interpretation is very free and his quotation of the Old Testament is not exact:

> I want you to notice, brethren, that our fathers were all under the cloud and all passed through the sea, and were all baptized in Moses' name in the cloud and in the sea, and all ate the same spiritual food, and all drank the same spiritual drink; for they drank from a spiritual rock that followed them, and the rock was Christ.

Here we notice not only the use of Christian terms to describe the spiritual experience of Israel, but also the use of nonbiblical elements in the story. In the Bible there is no rock which follows the Israelites. But the theory that such a rock existed is easy to explain on the basis of the biblical accounts. According to the three accounts of the miraculous gift of water (Exodus 17; Num. 20; 21:16ff.) the water was given at three different places. What could be more natural than to suppose, therefore, that the miracle was still more miraculous? The rock followed the Israelites. And so we find the story told in the Targum of Pseudo-Jonathan.[7] But the rock did not merely follow the Israelites; the rock was Christ. This idea has two possible sources. In the first place, to Paul Christ was the preexistent Wisdom of God, described in the Old Testament, which was God's instrument in the creation and providential care of the world. Now, according to Philo of Alexandria, the rock which gave forth water to the Israelites was to be identified with Wisdom. In the second place, in the Last Supper Christ gave spiritual food and drink to his disciples; this spiritual food and drink in his own body and blood; therefore the rock which gives spiritual drink must be identified with him. Is this exegesis arbitrary? The religious experience of Christians in their redemption from sin and death can be interpreted symbolically in terms of the saving of Israel from Egypt. And if the language of religion is naturally symbolic, we may find Paul's exegesis confirmed, not indeed by logic, but by the imaginative understanding which comes from faith.

With the mention of faith we come to what is perhaps the most important aspect of Paul's interpretation of the Old Testament. Why is it, he asks, that the Jews, to whom God originally gave the scriptures, cannot understand them as Christians do? Why do they not see the types and allegories which lie before them? His answer is set forth in the Second Epistle to the Corinthians. It is based on an Old Testament example. After Moses had spoken with God on Mount Sinai, his face shone so brightly that it was necessary for him to wear a veil with the children of Israel (Exodus 34):

> Until this very day the same veil remains, not taken away, in the reading of the Old Covenant; it is done away in Christ. Even to this day when Moses is read the veil lies on their heart; "but when he returns to the Lord, the veil will be taken off" [Exod. 34:34]. Now "the Lord" means the Spirit; and where the Spirit of the Lord is, there is freedom [2 Cor. 3:14ff.].

Here Moses is not only a type of the Old Testament but also a type of the unbelieving Israelite, who must return to the Lord as Moses did. Who is the Lord? He is the Spirit, who interprets the scriptures to the Christian heart, without a veil. The Spirit brings us freedom from the letter of the Old Testament. God has made us

> ministers of the New Covenant, not of the letter but of the Spirit; for the letter kills, but the Spirit makes alive [2 Cor. 3:6].

The letter is not the Old Testament as such; it is the Old Testament as a legal document, as the unconverted Israelites interpret it. By the aid of the Spirit we are able to understand the Old Testament as a spiritual book.[8]

The reason that others cannot thus understand the Old Testament is simply that they have not received the gift of the Spirit. They have been blinded, indeed blinded by Satan:

> If our gospel is hidden, it is hidden for those who are perishing, in whom the god of this age has blinded the minds of unbelievers, so that the light of the glorious gospel of Christ, who is the image of God, cannot shine [2 Cor. 4:3f.].

Here is the ultimate basis of Pauline exegesis. The true understanding of the Old Testament comes from God. Those who do not possess this true understanding have been blinded. Argument is possible, even argument on purely rational grounds (2 Cor. 4:2; cf. Rom. 2:15); but it can never convince those who do not share the gift of faith.

What shall we say of the form of Paul's exegesis? We have seen that its governing principles make it Christian; everything is finally determined by its reference to Christ. But in its outward aspects his interpretation of the Old Testament is not unlike the interpretation of some of his rabbinic contemporaries. Such similarities are what we should expect to find when we recall the statement in the Acts (22:3) that Paul was educated "at the feet of Gamaliel." And the analysis provided by the best modern scholars confirms this statement. Here we shall give only a few examples.

In the first place, Paul takes great liberties with the original meaning of passages he cites. The context means very little to him. Consider the quotation of Ps. 69:9 in Romans 15:3:

> Let each one of us please his neighbor for good, for edification; for even Christ did not please himself; but as it is written, "The reproaches of those who reproached you fell on me."

In the Gospel of John another part of the same verse is interpreted in reference to Christ: "Zeal for your house has consumed me" (John 2:17). While to us this may appear an improper use of a single verse out of a psalm which does not seem to be messianic, the early church found many messianic predictions in the psalms. And the rabbis often interpreted them in the same way. To one who knew the story of Christ's ministry, such exegesis would not seem arbitrary. And Paul goes on to justify his interpretation in the next verse of his letter:

> Whatever things were previously written were written for our instruction, in order that through patience and through the encouragement of the scriptures we might have hope.

This rabbinic principle is cited in order to justify characteristic rabbinic exegesis.

Another example of exegesis which is Christocentric in content and rabbinic in form is to be found in the first chapter of Colossians. Of Christ, Paul says:

> He is the image of the invisible God, the firstborn of all creation, for *in* him were created all things in the heavens and on the earth, the visible and the invisible, thrones, lordships, principalities, powers; all things were created *through* him and *for* him; and he is *before* all things, and all things have their consistency in him; and he is the head of the body, the Church; he is the beginning . . . [Col. 1:15ff.].

At first sight this passage appears to be a rhapsodic description of the preexistent Christ. But it is actually a typical result of rabbinic exegesis, with its underlying presuppositions stated only in part. Paul begins by recognizing Christ prefigured in Prov. 8:22, where Wisdom describes God's use of her in creation. Since Christ, the Wisdom of God, is God's agent in creation, we must naturally look for further light on his meaning in the creation story of Genesis. There it is stated that "in the beginning God made heaven and earth" (Gen. 1:1). The well-trained rabbinic interpreter will endeavor to define more closely the meaning of the preposition "in." Is it merely locative? Or does it not rather define the agency of creation? By comparing Prov. 8:22 we can see that it must describe the agency used by God, and we can express this still more clearly by replacing "in" with other prepositions, all of which seem to be applicable. "Through" this "beginning" and "for" him God made heaven and earth; he is "before" them and "with" them. One further deduction can be made from scripture: since in Paul's native tongue the same word means *beginning* and *head*, there is clearly pretypified the Christ who is not only the beginning of creation but head of his body, the Church.[9]

We may wonder at the way in which so imposing a structure is raised on what to us may seem so slight a foundation; and yet, given the general rule of Christocentric interpretation, as well as the rabbinic principle of the value of every word in scripture, the demonstration proceeds logically.

Perhaps the most instructive example of Christocentric interpretation, combined with verbal exegesis, is to be found in Rom. 10:5–10. Here, in the light of Paul's certitude of salvation by faith, he does not hesitate to analyze a passage of the Old Testament in which salvation by works is set forth, and to conclude that it proves salvation by faith! Moses writes (Lev. 18:5) that the man who does the righteousness which is of the Law shall live by it (Rom. 10:5). There is another passage in the Law which states that the performance of the Law is not impossible, or even difficult; and since this passage is contrary to Paul's own view (Romans 7) he finds that he must explain it away. The passage in Deuteronomy (30:11ff.) is as follows:

> For this commandment which I command thee this day, it is not too hard for thee, nor is it far off. It is not in heaven, that thou shouldst say, Who shall go up for us to heaven, and bring it to us, and make us hear it, that we may do it? Nor is it beyond the sea, that thou shouldst say, Who shall go over the sea for us, and bring it to us, and make us hear it, that we may do it? But the word is very near to thee, in thy mouth, and in thy heart, that thou mayst do it.

For the legal righteousness of the old covenant, Paul substitutes the righteousness of faith of the new covenant, and in true rabbinic fashion glosses each phrase to make it conform with his own thought.

> But the righteousness which is of faith speaks thus: Do not say in your heart, Who shall go up to heaven (*that is, to bring Christ down*) or, Who shall go down into the deep (*that is, to bring Christ up from the dead*)? But what does it say? The word is near thee, in thy mouth, and in thy heart (*that is, the word of faith which we preach*). For if you confess with your mouth Jesus as Lord, and believe in your heart that God raised him from the dead, you will be saved; for the heart's belief results in righteousness, and the mouth's confession results in salvation.

Paul believes that unless the Old Testament writer had Christ in mind, his expressions would be meaningless. For it is Christ who came down from heaven, who rose from the dead, who brought the gift of salvation. We may compare a similar exposition of Ps. 68:18 in the fourth chapter of Ephesians. In neither case are the *gesta Christi* obviously in the text; and as Bonsirven observes, "The strangest thing for us is that they (the examples of exegesis) take the form of a demonstration."[10]

These examples must suffice to show us the rabbinic form of Paul's exegesis of the Old Testament. The most striking feature of it is its verbalism, its emphasis on single words at the expense of contexts. And yet, as we have said, once we admit the Christocentric reference of the Old Testament we can understand it sympathetically. In the light of historical interpretation we should hesitate to insist on the permanent validity of the way in which Paul works out his interpretations. But for Christians the Old Testament is not a self-sufficient book. Its message is not complete. It looks forward beyond its own time to the coming of one who we believe came in Jesus.

When we have examined instances of Christian rabbinism in Paul's letters we have not finished our task. It is obvious that there is a striking difference between their work and his. He writes in Greek. The significance of this fact must not be overvalued; there was much Greek in Jewish Palestine; and Greek philosophical thought persistently influenced Judaism. We should, however, compare Paul's exegesis with that of another Jew who wrote in the Greek language. And we shall find a few remarkable similarities between the exegetical work of Paul and that of Philo of Alexandria.

Paul's emphasis on the singular "seed" in Gal. 3:16 finds a parallel in Philo's stress on the singular "child" in Gen. 17:16 (*De mut. nom.* 145); again, both Paul and Philo find hidden meanings in names, especially the names of persons important in biblical history. Both Paul and Philo allegorize the name of Hagar (Galations 4; *Leg. alleg.* 3.244). A more important example is to be found in Paul's identification of the miraculous rock with Christ; Philo identifies it with Wisdom or the Logos (*Leg. alleg.* 2.86; *Quod det. pot.* 118).

Perhaps we may not agree with Michel's conclusion that in spite of differences the exegesis of Philo is closer to that of Paul than is that of the rabbis. But we can make his suggestion our own, that both Philo and Paul are dependent on the exegetical tradition of the Hellenistic synagogue.[11] Both differ from the rabbinic exegetical tradition, however, in their outlook. For both Philo and Paul are apostles to the gentiles. Both Philo and Paul make use of the terminology of Greek rhetoric.

Yet Paul cannot be explained merely in terms of his Jewish and Greek sources. His whole personality was changed by his experience of conversion. It is possible that like other converts he somewhat exaggerated the extent of the change; but, it is true, especially in regard to his view of the Old Testament, that it is no longer he who lives, but Christ who lives in him (Gal. 2:20). He has died to the Law, through the Law, that he may live to God (Gal. 2:19). His interpretation of scripture cannot possibly be what it was in his pre-Christian life. The Old Testament remains scripture; but it is no longer letter, but Spirit; no longer Law, but a ministry of grace. And in it everywhere is Christ; for Christ is the end of the Law (Rom. 10:4) and we now serve in newness of the Spirit, and not in oldness of the letter (Rom. 7:6). A specifically Christian interpretation of the Old Testament has come into existence.

4

The Old Testament
in the New

We have observed the way in which the apostle Paul develops his Christocentric interpretation of the Old Testament. But the Pauline epistles do not present it in its final form. The examples of exegesis which we find in them have an air of freedom. We cannot be sure that if Paul had interpreted the same passage twice he would have interpreted it the same way. He makes use of ad hoc interpretations. In the epistle to the Hebrews, on the other hand, there is a carefully worked out, allusive type of exegesis which takes a passage of scripture and is not content to rest until the last subtlety of meaning has been extracted from it.

One reason for this difference is to be found in the character of the audience to which the epistle is addressed. It is not intended for recent enthusiastic converts; it is written for those who have been Christians for a long time and are tiring of the effort. They know their Old Testament. It is possible that they know it too well. The epistle opens with a magnificent rhetorical statement of the inadequacy and incompleteness of the revelation in the Old Testament, and of the finality of the revelation in God's Son (Heb. 1:1–3). Then the author turns abruptly to a series of prooftexts designed to show on the one hand the superiority of the Son to the angels, and on the other hand their inferiority to him. Why is this necessary? The answer seems to lie in the fact that the eighth psalm was taken messianically, with reference to Christ. And while it says, "Thou has set everything under his feet"—this is the line quoted by Paul in 1 Cor. 15:27—it also says of the "son of man," "Thou has made him a little lower than the angels." Psalm readers, especially those familiar with angelologies like the one favored at Qumran, might easily conclude that Jesus was inferior to the angels. The author of Hebrews opposes such an idea, first by giving a series of proofs from scripture which show that Jesus is superior to the angels (Heb. 1:5–13) and second by carefully examining Psalm 8, stressing the phrases which point to Jesus' glorification and emphasizing the transitoriness of his subjection (2:5–10). From this example alone we can conclude with Scott that the author's method of exegesis

> consists not so much in attentuating the letter of scripture as in emphasising it—examining it, so to speak, under the microscope, in order to ascertain its full implication.[1]

In the manner of the Qumran sectarians he begins by applying an Old Testament passage directly to the new situation. He goes further than they did, however. Ultimately, the complete reality of the Old Testament is denied in Hebrews; the Law had only a shadow of the good things to come, not the living image of them (Heb. 10:1). It is faith which provides them with substance (11:1).

There are two great examples in which the author of Hebrews sees typified the person and work of Christ. These are the mysterious Melchizedek, priest-king of Salem (Gen. 14:17ff.; Hebrews 7), and the work of the Levitical priesthood as a whole (Hebrews 8—10). In the first place, contemporary Christian usage of the messianic Psalm 110 encourages our author to make his microscopic investigation of its details. Where earlier Christians had quoted only the first verse of the psalm, he now applies the fourth verse directly to Jesus: "Thou are a priest for ever, after the order of Melchizedek." After quoting part of the story of Melchizedek from Genesis, the author of Hebrews goes on to explain his significance as a type. He was king of righteousness and king of peace, for etymologically (according to our author) Melchizedek means "king of righteousness" and Salem, "peace." The meaning of these names is significant, for Isaiah has predicted that the coming Savior would be called the "prince of peace" (Isa. 9:6f.). By means of such a passage Jesus can be shown to have been foreshadowed in Melchizedek.[2]

It is not simply a question of names which is involved here, however, Melchizedek is such a mysterious figure in the Old Testament that his meaning can be investigated more fully. Unlike the other personages of the Old Testament story he has no family history. He suddenly appears and as suddenly disappears. Therefore the author of Hebrews can find in him a type of the eternal Christ, who was also "without father, without mother, without genealogy, having neither beginning of days nor end of life" (Heb. 7:3). Furthermore, Melchizedek's priesthood is of a higher rank than that of Levi; for Melchizedek blessed Abraham after tithing him. It is obvious that the inferior person is blessed by the superior (7:7). And in Abraham's payment to Melchizedek we see a tithe paid, not to Levi or the Levitical priesthood, but by Levi, who was "in his father's loins" (7:10). We have proved the superiority of the Melchizedekan priesthood to the Levitical. Indeed, Jesus, our great high priest, does not belong to the Levitical priesthood; there is no prophecy in the writings of Moses concerning a priest to rise from the tribe of Judah (7:14). The prophecy which he fulfills is the story of Melchizedek.

In a summary of his understanding of Jesus as a priest after the order of Melchizedek, our author concludes his portrayal of the person of Christ in the Old Testament and passes on to consider his work:

> To summarize what we have said, we have such a high priest, who is seated at the right hand of the throne of majesty in heaven, a minister of holy things and of the true tabernacle which the Lord, not man, set up. For every high priest is appointed to offer gifts and sacrifices; therefore it is necessary that he too have something to offer [Heb. 8:1–3].

Evidently the author has begun with the traditional Christian interpretation of Ps. 110:1 as related to Jesus and has read on in the psalm, finding further theological relevance in the fourth verse, in which he has encountered the mysterious figure of Melchizedek. The parallels he draws do not prove anything. They simply add richness to the Christian view of the Christocentric meaning of the Old Testament, and make Melchizedek more meaningful. Such an interpretation our author calls a "parable," or comparison (Heb. 11:19; cf. 9:9). An additional comparison which he might well have made is between Melchizedek's bringing forth bread and wine (Gen. 14:18) and the bringing forth of bread and wine by Jesus at the Last Supper. Perhaps he regards this as too holy to mention. Perhaps, on the other hand, his interest is so completely absorbed in his other comparisons that he cannot here discuss it. As is often the case in typological exegesis, the author removes Melchizedek entirely from his historical setting. Moreover, he does not really understand the sacrificial cultus. But these shortcomings do not destroy the value of his work for us. We may prefer other procedures, but we should hesitate to deny the religious value of the results.

The other example is the work of the Levitical priesthood. When the author of Hebrews turns to consider the work of Jesus, he regards it as the ministry of a covenant which is eternal as well as new. The earthly ministry of the Mosaic priesthood is merely a copy of this true and heavenly ministry, for in Exod. 25:40 God instructs Moses to "make all things according to the pattern which was shown thee on the mountain." This pattern is the heavenly prefiguration of the earthly copy. Everything in the earthly copy has special significance; but here the author is concentrating his attention only on the most important correspondences (Heb. 9:5):

> Christ having come as a high priest of the good things to come, through the greater and more perfect tabernacle, not made with hands, that is to say, not of this creation, nor yet through the blood of goats and calves, entered in once for all into the holy place, having obtained eternal redemption [Heb. 9:11f.].

Under the old covenant the high priest alone went into the Holy of Holies, and only once a year. He had to offer repeated sacrifices of the blood of calves and goats. These sacrifices had to be renewed year after year. And they were made, not only for the people, but also for the sins of the high priest himself. But under the new covenant, Jesus entered once for all into the true Holy of Holies, which is heaven (Heb. 9:24). His sacrifice is his own blood, for "it is impossible that the blood of bulls and goats should take away sins" (10:4). And while he did not offer his blood as a sacrifice for his own sin, for he was without sin, he was made perfect only by his obedience which resulted in his death (4:15; 5:9). And "by one offering he has forever perfected those who are sanctified" (10: 14). He has opened a way for them into the true Holy of Holies, heaven, through the veil, which was his flesh (10:20).

As scholars have often observed, the picture which is drawn for us in Hebrews is hardly a complete or even an accurate picture of the meaning of sacrifice in the Old Testament. But the author is not really concerned with the Old Testament as a source book for history or archaeology. He is looking for examples which will support his own theory of the meaning of Jesus' sacrifice. To his mind, the Christocentric interpretation of scripture alone gives meaning to the Old Testament. And in the eleventh chapter of his treatise he tells the story of Israel as it must be understood in the light of the revelation of Christ. The patriarchs and the prophets all looked forward to the fulfillment of its coming by the faith that was in them. Without faith the Old Testament history is no history, but a collection of fragments. By means of the key of faith the author of Hebrews finds in it a "cloud of witnesses" who like Christians look to Jesus, the author and perfecter of our faith (Heb. 12:2).

What is the relation of our author's exegesis to that of his predecessors? It is far more carefully worked out than that of Paul. Where the apostle to the gentiles writes with frequent offhand allusions to numerous verses of scripture which he recalls from memory, the author of Hebrews rigorously revolves a few selected texts and examines their reciprocal relations. His analysis of the high-priesthood of Jesus is ultimately based on only two texts, Psalm 110 and the description in Genesis of Melchizedek. His portrayal of Christ's work is constructed almost entirely out of the accounts of temple cultus in the Pentateuch. His knowledge of the Old Testament, at the same time, is somewhat superficial when it is compared with that of Paul. He does not live in the thought-world of the Old Testament as Paul does. But to him, just as to the contemporary author of 1 Peter, the human life of Jesus means a great deal. He knows the "prayers and supplications with strong crying and tears" which Jesus offered up (Heb. 5:7); he knows that Jesus was tempted but did not yield (4:15); he knows of his death outside the gate of Jerusalem (13:12); and he knows that he came from the tribe of Judah (7:14). Evidently there is a story which lies behind these isolated fragments. Had the author of Hebrews intended to write a gospel, we might have had a work like the Gospel of John. It would have combined historical reminiscences with interpretations of Jesus' meaning in the light of the Old Testament and of Christian experience. But Hebrews is not a gospel; it is a detailed analysis of the Christocentric meaning of the Old Testament. The true meaning of the Old Testament is to be found only in Christ. In fact, there is no other meaning. The Law had only a shadow of the good things to come, not the very image of the things (Heb. 10:1).

The epistle to the Hebrews played an important role in the history of exegesis. It encouraged the fancifulness of allegorists and others who sought for hidden meanings in the Old Testament. At the same time it achieved more positive results. Without the typological method it would have been almost impossible for the early church to retain its grasp on the Old Testament.

While the epistle to the Hebrews represents the most thorough analysis of the Old Testament in typological terms which we possess in the New Testament, there are many other examples of typology. As we have seen, the early church was intensely interested in the ways in which the life of Jesus was prefigured in the Old Testament. We are not surprised, therefore, to find this interest in gospel stories.

It has often been observed that the evangelist Matthew stands close to the rabbis of Palestine in his devotion to the Old Testament. The Christians for whom he writes have to be warned in Jesus' name not to let themselves be called "rabbi" (Matt. 23:8). And while we might prefer to believe that Jesus' word concerning the "fulfillment" of the Law (Matt. 5:17) refers to the completeness and finality of his ethical teaching, Matthew himself evidently takes it as a reference to Jesus' fulfillment of the prophecies of scripture. A *yodh* or a corner of a letter shall not pass away from the Law—until everything takes place (Matt. 5:18).

Almost everything in Jesus' life takes place "in order that it might be fulfilled"; the prophecies of scripture (and all scripture can be understood as prophecy) have a direct reference to him. His virginal conception fulfilled Isa. 7:14 (according to the Greek version): "Behold, a virgin shall conceive" (Matt. 1:23). He was born in Bethlehem because a combination of Mic. 5:1 and 3, and 2 Sam. 5:2 pointed to the exaltation of Bethlehem and the birth of a shepherd king (Matt. 2:6). Hosea foretold his return from Egypt when he said (Hos. 11:1): "Out of Egypt have I called my son" (Matt. 2:15). He came to live in Nazareth because it was said "through the prophets" that he would be called a Nazarene (Matt. 2:23). It is evident from these examples that the choice of passage to prove the origin of Jesus in Nazareth had been mislaid when Matthew wrote. Similarly, in quoting from memory a prophecy of the thirty pieces of silver (Matt. 27:9) Matthew ascribes it to Jeremiah rather than to Zechariah. But these errors are exceptions to the ordinary carefulness of his research.

This method of exegesis is not, of course, original with Matthew. Jesus himself had been aware of the correspondences between his mission and some of the prophecies of scripture, and in the Gospel of Mark there are references to the "beginning of the gospel" in Mal. 3:1 and Isa. 40:3 (Mark 1:2f.), as well as to the sufferings and death of Jesus foretold by the prophets. Paul, as we have seen, made use of the typology of the Old Testament, and observed the resemblances between the Exodus of the old Israel and the salvation of the church. But Matthew is more thoroughgoing than his predecessors. Where Paul only alludes to the superiority of Christ to Moses, the epistle to the Hebrews makes the comparison explicit, and in the Gospel of Matthew the portrayal of Christ as the new Moses is complete.[3]

In the first place, Christ gives the new Law on a new mountaintop (Matt. 5:1); from another mountain (or is it the same?) he sends his disciples forward into the new promised land (Matt. 28:16ff.). As at the birth of Moses, the whole house was filled with light,[4] so now a star guides magi to Jesus' birthplace. As the king of Egypt tried to kill Moses and destroyed the other infants, so Herod tries to kill Jesus and slaughters the innocents of Bethlehem and its vicinity. Like Moses, Jesus came out of the land of Egypt. And as Moses was transfigured on the mount, so also Jesus was transfigured. Here there are too many similarities for all of them to be coincidental. Matthew is firmly convinced that Jesus is the new Moses who came to bring a new Law. And he is determined to prove this fact to others by the use of Old Testament prophecy.

It is not only the Jewish evangelist Matthew who makes use of the Old Testament for proof of the divine fulfillment of prophecy;

the same task is undertaken by the gentile Luke. As Lestringant observes:

> No page of Matthew bears the imprint of the vocation of the elect people as strongly as the beginning of St. Luke. The Magnificat, the canticles of Zachariah and of Simeon present us with the gift made to Israel as an accomplished fact. At the other end of his narrative, the risen Christ twice reproaches the disciples for their slowness in understanding the scriptures; he opens their spirit and explains to them what concerns him in the Pentateuch, in the Prophets, and in the Psalms [Luke 24:25–47].[5]

In the course of the life of Jesus, however, Luke is much less concerned than Matthew to demonstrate the fulfillment of a prophecy of scripture by each incident. He is content to set the stage and to bring down the curtain.

The evangelist John is more subtly related to the Old Testament. He does not provide many actual quotations from scripture; he more often alludes to the Old Testament in passing. The Old Testament provides him with themes for some of the long sermons which in the name of the Spirit he ascribes to Christ. But he is aware, as he states in the prologue to his Gospel, that when the true Light shone forth to its people through the prophets, the people did not receive it. There were a few who did receive it, who were given power to become the children of God. Finally, however, there was a complete revelation in the tabernacle of the flesh (John 1:14), and this was far superior to the revelation which had been given before. "The Law was given through Moses, but grace and truth came through Jesus Christ" (1:17). No one has ever seen God; the divine Son has revealed him (1:18). Isaiah said that he saw the Lord of hosts (Isa. 6:5); actually he saw the glory of the preexistent Christ (John 12:41). The only meaning of the Old Testament is prophetic (5:46; cf. Rev. 19:10).

The exegetical outlook of the New Testament writings as a whole does not differ greatly from that of the writings we have already mentioned. The pastoral epistles apparently were composed late in the first century to set forth Pauline doctrine adapted to a new situation. The rather highly developed form of ecclesiastical government reflected by the pastorals suggests that they do not come from within the lifetime of Paul; and their teaching concerning scripture is more systematic than his. Paul is represented as commending Timothy for his lifelong knowledge of the holy writings, "which can instruct you for salvation through the faith which is in Christ Jesus":

All scripture is inspired and helpful for instruction *or* Every inspired scripture is helpful for instruction [2 Tim. 3:16].

In either case, Paul is represented as emphasizing the value of the Old Testament. Timothy is expected to resist those who "desire to be teachers of law," however; the Law is good, but it must be used lawfully; it requires interpretation (1 Tim. 1:7f.). Timothy must also avoid "myths and endless genealogies" (1 Tim. 1:4) or, as they are elsewhere called, "Jewish myths and human commandments" (Titus 1:14). Are not the interpretations of Timothy's opponents the two divisions of Jewish exegesis? The "myths and genealogies" are the *haggada*, interpretations of a theological rather than a legal nature; the "human commandments" are the *halaka*, rules regulating conduct.[6]

The so-called Second Epistle of Peter also deals with the problem of biblical interpretation. Its author knows those who "twist" the letters of Paul and the other scriptures (2 Pet. 3:15f.), and he is confronted by critics who ask, "Where is the promise of his coming?" (2 Pet. 3:4). Another passage is unfortunately obscure, except for its conclusion, which states emphatically that the prophets were inspired by the Holy Spirit (2 Pet. 1:20f.). By later defenders of ecclesiastical authority it was read, "No prophecy of scripture is of private interpretation," but this does not seem to be its real meaning.

In conclusion we may say that the New Testament method of interpreting the Old was generally that of typology. Types and prophecies of the coming of Christ were sought throughout the Old Testament and, with the life of Christ already known to all, they were readily found. Only tentative statements of a theory of typology are set forth. But had the earliest Christians been interested in theory, it is likely that they would have expressed themselves much as Justin does.

Sometimes the Holy Spirit caused what was to be a type of the future to be performed openly, and sometimes he also uttered sayings about things which were to happen in the future as though they were then taking place, or had already taken place. And unless readers know this method they will not be able to follow the words of the prophets as they ought [*Dial.* 114:1; cf. 1 Pet. 1:10–12].

With this preestablished harmony between the Old Testament and the words of Jesus, the Old Testament could become an armory of prooftexts. And while it can doubtless be said that Jesus was the one to whom the prophets looked forward, it is by no means so certain, even to the eye of faith, that the Pentateuch and the Psalms predict his coming. Their primary reference is clearly to the events of past and present which they describe.

The typological method is based on the presupposition that the whole Old Testament looks beyond itself for its interpretation. Just as the prophets made predictions, so the other Old Testament writers wrote what they wrote with a view to the future. Obviously there is some justification for this presupposition. The Old Testament writers did not record past events because they were fascinated with the past as such; they wrote because the past events had present significance, and future significance as well. They believed that the God who was working in their own times and would work in the times to come was the same God who had worked hitherto. They had what we might call an "existential concern" with the history of God's acts. Christian exegetes, believing that the God of the Old Testament was the Father of Jesus who had raised him from the dead, could not fail to regard God's working as continuous and consistent. They therefore regarded the events described in the Old Testament as prefigurations of events in the life of Jesus and of his church.

Difficulties arise at points where the resemblances are based upon parallels merely verbal, or where contexts are ignored. These difficulties are the fault of individual exegetes, however, not of the typological method as such.[7] Imagination has to be restrained by common sense, not killed by it.

We should also point out, after E. Stauffer[8] and others, that the evangelist John provides clear warrant for looking beyond the New

Testament itself for exegesis not only of the Old Testament but also of the gospel: (1) The Christian tradition contained more about Jesus than what was written down either by John (20:30–31) or by other evangelists (21:25). (2) Jesus had more to say to his disciples than what he said during his ministry (16:12; cf. 14:25). (3) The Spirit was to come to the disciples, to teach them and remind them of all that Jesus had said (14:26), and to guide them into all the truth (16:13).

5

The Bible
in the Second Century

For the writers whom we have been considering, the only written source of authority, the only book which could be called *scripture*, was the Old Testament. In the light of the principle, inherited from Judaism, that God's will in its entirety was to be found expressed in the Old Testament, no further authoritative document was necessary. This is clearly shown in the Acts of the Apostles, where the constant reference of early Christians is to the Old Testament for theological understanding and there is only one allusion to "the words of the Lord Jesus, how he said . . ." (Acts 20:35). But after the earliest days of Christianity it became necessary to write down and carefully preserve not only the sayings but also the deeds of Jesus. Apparently the first element of the tradition to be set down in writing was the passion narrative, the story of the sufferings and death of Christ. In the epistles of Paul, as well as in 1 Peter and Hebrews, there are fairly frequent references to it. Then with this narrative were combined collections of the sayings of Jesus which had previously circulated only in oral form.

The first impetus to the collection of the group of books which was to become a "New Testament" was not, however, given by the writing of gospels. According to a theory originally developed by E. J. Goodspeed, the "publication" of the Acts of the Apostles led to fresh interest in the letters of Paul, and towards the end of the first century they were collected, probably in Asia Minor. The Epistle to the Ephesians—actually an encyclical treatise—was composed by a Paulinist in order to reinterpret the thought of Paul for a somewhat later day. Whether this theory be correct or not, it cannot be denied that at the end of the first century we find widespread knowledge of the Pauline epistles among Christians. We also find that some of the gospels are well known. Neither epistles nor gospels, however, are regarded as scripture. The Old Testament remains the sacred book of the church.

Some light on the obscure and tantalizing situation may perhaps be shed by a difficult passage in the letters of Ignatius, bishop of Antioch, early in the second century. In writing to the church of Philadelphia, Ignatius apparently finds Christians who are so devoted to the Old Testament that they can say, "If I do not find it in the 'charters' I do not believe in the gospel." Ignatius' reply is this: "It is written in scripture." But they answer sharply: "That is just the question." Ignatius, whose quotations from the Old Testament are very infrequent, goes on to state that for him the "charters" are Jesus Christ and his saving works and the faith which comes through him; he desires to be "justified" by these (*Philad.* 8.2). Though he knows some of the New Testament books (certainly 1 Corinthians and other Pauline epistles, probably John, possibly Matthew and Luke), he does not appeal to them at this point, for the question his opponents have raised is that of the Christological interpretation of the Old Testament. It is significant that they do not seem to accept it. Ignatius' own view is clear: the Old Testament prophets lived "according to Christ Jesus" (*Magn.* 8.2).

While the situation is not altogether clear at the beginning of the second century, by the time of the pseudonymous Second Epistle of Peter it is more distinct. 2 Peter is probably the latest book of our New Testament. It is written in a time when the eschatological hope has begun to seem mistaken and when the spontaneous expressions of Paul are being misunderstood. This misunderstanding is all the more important because the letters of Paul have come to be regarded as scripture:

There are some things in them hard to understand, which ignorant, unsteadfast people twist to their own ruin, just as they do the rest of the scriptures [2 Pet. 3:16].

The expression "the rest of the scriptures" shows plainly that the Pauline epistles—including, perhaps, 1 Timothy (1:16)—also have been regarded as scripture by "Peter" and those for whom he writes. And while he does not explicitly quote from the Old Testament, his allusions to it are sufficient to show that he regards it as scripture too. In addition, it is probable that in 2 Peter 1:17–18 he refers to the Gospel of Mark as the source of his account of the Transfiguration. 2 Peter reflects the situation of many ordinary Christian communities in the early second century. The Old Testament is scripture; but the gospels probably and the epistles certainly are scripture as well.

The Christian church in the second century was full of variety, however, and there were many leaders of Christian thought who did not share such a view. We find a wide range of opinion in regard to the place of the Old Testament in the church. In the epistle of Barnabas, for example, the attempt is made to show that the Old Testament has meaning only when it is understood in terms of the gospel. The author's theme is not new, but his exegetical method is characterized by a somewhat perverse typology. To him history is really meaningless. God's covenant has always been made with us Christians. There is here no analysis of the relation of the old covenant to the new; there is the simple assertion that the Old Testament has always been misunderstood by the Jews:

> Take heed to yourselves now, and be not made like some, heaping up your sins and saying that the covenant is both theirs and ours. It is ours [Barnabas 4:6f.].

Here Barnabas' typological exegesis leads him to the rejection not only of Old Testament history but also of the general Christian understanding of the meaning of that history. As Windisch has observed, he is not far from the heretical Gnosticism of the second century.[1] And the eccentricity of his exegesis, especially in the celebrated example of the 318 servants of Abraham,[2] does not increase our respect for his intelligence.

A second-century Christian who did not share Barnabas' enthusiasm for typology, and at the same time rejected the claims of Judaism, might well deny the need for retaining the Old Testament. This denial was proposed as the true interpretation of Christian faith by Marcion of Pontus. It has sometimes been claimed that in the second century Marcion alone understood the thought of the apostle Paul. But while Paul was Marcion's hero, hero worship and comprehension are not the same thing; Marcion's attitude towards the Old Testament could have horrified the apostle. A reading of Romans 9—11 makes this point clear. To Paul's brethren, the Israelites, belong the adoption and the glory and the covenants and the giving of the Law and the service of God and the promises. The patriarchs are theirs, and so is Christ "after the flesh" (Rom. 9:4f.). On the one hand, they are enemies of God for your sake; on the other, they are beloved by him for their fathers' sake, for God never repents of his gifts or his calling (11:28f.). Paul is fully aware of the difficulty and the depth of his theme: "O the depth of the riches both of the wisdom and of the knowledge of God! how unsearchable his judgments, how inscrutable his ways!" (11:33). But Marcion forgets the glory of Israel in his insistence upon its enmity to God; and for him there is no mystery in its rejection.

To understand Marcion's attitude towards the Old Testament it is necessary to observe that it is based on a thoroughgoing dualism. Marcion endeavored to interpret Pauline thought in the light of his own view that there are two gods: the just God of the Law, who created the world and is the God of the Jews; and the good God, who is the Father of Jesus Christ. This is not the impression of Christian doctrine which an unprejudiced reading of the New Testament would give, and indeed Marcion was able to show that his view was based on the New Testament only by drastically criticizing the text. The Pauline epistles had been interpolated, he found; and by correcting them he found also that they could be made to speak his language. Of the gospels only that according to Luke was in any way genuine, and it had been interpolated. Even in its pure state it required a commentary before it could be shown to speak the authentic gospel. And in his *Antitheses* Marcion provided such a commentary, on both the gospel and what he called "the apostle." This commentary, occasionally quoted by Tertullian in his fourth and fifth books against Marcion, is ordinarily literal. It interprets the gospel, as Harnack observes, by reference to the chief points of Romans and Galatians. Tertullian's judgment on it is too sharp: "he would rather call a passage an addition than explain it" (*Adv. Marc.* 4.7); for the method which Marcion used was the ordinary text criticism of the poets.[3] Apart from a few obviously strained interpretations in which Marcion tries to introduce his theory of two gods or of a phantomlike Jesus, his exegesis is sober and literal. He stresses the novelty of the gospel and the fact that it is addressed to all nations. He observes that many of the original disciples misunderstood it. But his final interpretation of the gospel shows to what lengths his theory could lead. The Gospel of Luke (24:39) represents the risen Jesus as showing his disciples his fleshly body, and observing, "A spirit does not have flesh and bones, such as you see me having." Marcion is certain that this passage is misunderstood. He prefers to read, "A spirit, such as you see me having, does not have flesh and bones" (*Adv. Marc.* 4.43)!

Marcion not only rejected the Old Testament as a Christian book; he insisted on a literal interpretation of it in order to emphasize its crudity. It was not a Christian book, and in his opinion no allegorical exegesis could make it one. Jesus destroyed the prophets and the Law (Irenaeus, *Adv. haer.* 1.27.2, 1, 217 Harvey). An interesting example of the rigor of Marcion's logic is to be found in his analysis of the *Descensus ad Inferos*. Jesus preached to the dead of Israel, but he received a mixed hearing. Cain, the men of Sodom, the Egyptians, in fact all kinds of evildoers were saved by him, for they came to him and were received into his kingdom; but all the righteous, including the patriarchs and the prophets, were not saved. They believed that as usual God was testing them. Here is justification by faith only, with a vengeance! With this kind of exegesis no value could be placed on the Old Testament.

A story told by Epiphanius (*Pan.* 42.2, 2, 95f. Holl) illustrates Marcion's attitude toward the interpretation of the New Testament. He asked the elders of the Roman church to explain the sayings in the gospel about new wine and old wineskins and about the patch on a garment. He was told, not unjudiciously, that the old wineskins represent the hearts of the Pharisees and the scribes, and somewhat less judiciously, that the old garment on which the patch was placed was Judas Iscariot. Marcion was quite unwilling to accept these interpretations. And it must be admitted that many of his contemporaries had lost their sense of the newness of Christianity. They had forgotten its radical difference from what had come before. Nevertheless for his part he had failed to preserve a proper sense of the continuity of the Christian message with its intimations in Israel. In this sense even the typological absurdities of

Barnabas are more satisfactory. For they make plain the fact that without the Old Testament there could not have been a New.

One of the earliest writers against Marcion, one who was also a leader in the Christian apologetic movement, was Justin Martyr.[4] In his thought we see foreshadowed what was to become the classical Christian teaching concerning the Old Testament. Unlike Marcion, Justin rejects the idea of a radical cleavage between Christianity and the rest of God's witness in the world. He holds that all God's witness can be called Christianity. He claims that even such philosophers as Socrates and Heraclitus truly deserve the name "Christian" (1 *Apol*. 46.3, 58 Goodspeed). For Justin there is a difference only of degree between God's revelation in the Old Testament and the highest Greek philosophy, and that in Christ. He constantly emphasizes the pedagogical role of the Logos, whether among the prophets and philosophers or incarnate in Jesus Christ, "our teacher."

Justin's understanding of the meaning of the Old Testament is set forth at great length in his *Dialogue with Trypho*. This book purports to be the record of two days' discourse between Justin and a learned rabbi of the second century. Each tries to convert the other, and the upshot is a fairly amicable agreement to disagree. The occasion of the dialogue is represented as being given by Trypho's advice to Justin to "be circumcised, then (as is commanded in the Law) keep the Sabbath and the feasts and God's new moons, and in short, do all the things that are written in the Law, and then perhaps you will find mercy from God." In opposition to the Christian belief, he adds that "Messiah, if indeed he has ever been and now exists anywhere, is unknown, and does not even know himself at all, and has no power until Elijah has come and anointed him and made him manifest to all" (*Dial*. 8.4).

The Christian apologist has to provide a thorough analysis of the relevance of the Law for Christians. Justin, while relying on earlier insights, sets forth an exegesis of the Old Testament which is at once Christocentric and historical. He does not deny the historical reality of God's relationship to Israel, but he insists that the earlier covenant itself looks forward to being superseded.

He shows from the writing of the prophets that they looked forward to a new covenant with God which would take the place of the earlier one. The patriarchs were saved without circumcision, sabbath keeping, or observance of the laws concerning food and sacrifices. Moreover, regarding the Messiah, the Old Testament itself proves that there were to be two advents, one in humility, in which he would be rejected—this has already taken place—and one in glory, which is still in the future. By many passages of scripture, understood typologically, Justin shows that Jesus was this expected Messiah. Some of his best proofs, he charges, have been removed from the scriptures by the Jews (*Dial.* 72f.).

But what kind of "proof" does he give? An unfortunate example of his mode of argument is to be found in *Dial.* 77f.

> *Trypho:* I ask you to prove the passage of scripture (Isa. 7:14) which you have often promised . . . for we say that it was prophesied of Hezekiah.
>
> *Justin:* First you prove to me that the following words were spoken of Hezekiah . . . "Before the child knows how to call father or mother, he shall take the power of Damascus and the spoils of Samaria in the presence of the king of Assyria" (Isa. 8:4). You cannot prove that this has ever happened to anyone among the Jews, but we can prove that it took place in the case of our Christ. For at the very time that he was born magi came from Arabia and worshipped him, after they had first been to Herod . . . whom the Word calls king of Assyria because of his godless and lawless mind. For you know that the Holy Spirit often speaks things of this kind in parables and similitudes. . . . For that saying of Isaiah meant that the power of the devil, who dwelt at Damascus, should be overcome by Christ at his very birth. And this proved to have taken place. For the magi, who had been carried off as spoil for all kinds of evil actions, which were wrought in them by that demon, by coming and worshipping Christ are shown to have departed from that power which had taken them as spoil, which the word signified to us in a mystery as dwelling in Damascus. And that very power, as being sinful and wicked, he rightly calls Samaria in a parable. Now that Damascus did and does belong to the land of Arabia . . . none of you can deny.

It would be difficult to claim that there is much logic in this proof, or even much intuition. Justin's lack of enthusiasm for Samaria is perhaps due to the fact that he was born there.[5] But to think that all this nonsense really proves that the prophecy of a miraculous birth refers to Jesus is very hard! It is typology run riot. A much sounder interpretation, in general, is given us later by Irenaeus. But we must not forget that Justin and others of similar exegetical habits preserved the Old Testament for the Christian church.

A much more systematic analysis of the meaning of the Old Testament is the *Letter to Flora* of the Valentinian Ptolemaeus, preserved by Epiphanius in his *Panarion* (*Pan.* 33.5ff., 1, 450ff. Holl).[6] It is a clear, calm, nonpolemical theological treatise, intended to lead "Flora"—perhaps the Roman Church—down the path towards the garden of Valentinian Gnosticism, primarily by emphasizing ideas which the more orthodox could share with Gnostics. The fundamental source of authoritative teaching to which Ptolemaeus appeals is found in "the words of our Savior, by which alone one can be led without error to the knowledge of things." Then follows a clear and precise treatment of the Law as it can be understood from the teaching of Jesus: "First of all, it is to be known that the entire Law contained in the Pentateuch of Moses was not given by one—I mean not by God alone; but some of its teachings were given by men, and the words of the Savior teach us to divide it into three parts." These parts are as follows:

> He attributes some of it to God himself and his legislation, and some to Moses, not in the sense that God gave laws through him, but in the sense that Moses, impelled by his own spirit, set down some things as laws; and he attributes some things to the elders of the people, who first discovered certain commandments of their own and then inserted them. How this was so you may clearly learn from the words of the Savior.

Then follows a proof of these statements taken from the words of Jesus from the synoptic tradition.

The most important part of the Law, of course, is the part given by God himself, and this Ptolemaeus again subdivides, also into three parts:

> First, into the genuine precepts, quite untainted with evil, which are properly called the Law, which the Savior came not to destroy but to fulfill [Matt. 5:17] . . . , second, the part comprising evil and unrighteous things, which the Savior did away with as something unfitting his nature; and third, that part which is typical and symbolical,

given as a law after the image of things spiritual and more excellent; this is the Savior transformed from sensible and visible into spiritual and invisible. Now the Law of God, pure and uncompromising, is the Decalogue. . . . Although they constitute a pure body of laws, they are not perfect, and they need to be completed by the Savior.

Other regulations are mixed with evil, such as the laws upholding vengeance; here, relying on the Sermon on the Mount, Ptolemaeus observes that these commandments violate the pure Law (Matt. 5:38). And the final part of the Law of God is the typical part; all the regulations of Jewish cultus now have a spiritual meaning, as Paul clearly shows when he says, "Christ our Passover is sacrificed for us" (1 Cor. 5:7). The analysis which Ptolemaeus gives is acute and even subtle, and it will repay detailed study. Here we can notice only its most striking features. It has the merit of being systematic. It is also traditional. Ptolemaeus emphasizes the fact that he has received the truth from an apostolic succession (of Gnostics). And it is Christocentric. Like his more orthodox contemporaries, Ptolemaeus lays great stress not only on the teaching of Jesus but also on his being foreshadowed in the Old Testament. We should not, however, overlook his basic purpose—the conversion of Flora to Valentinianism.[7]

We should not make the mistake of considering Ptolemaeus a modern scholar. His emphasis in the *Letter to Flora* is not the emphasis which we find in his teaching as set forth by Irenaeus. He was a Valentinian, and his exegesis could be fantastic. The insights which we find in this letter are largely to be found also in Irenaeus, and in general Irenaeus' interpretation of scripture is sounder. He does not have to distort his documents so much to get them to express his views. Of course, this distortion is not to be found in the *Letter to Flora*; but another example of Ptolemaeus' exegesis, based on the prologue to the Gospel of John, reveals him as a highly imaginative writer.

Ptolemaeus differs from most of his contemporaries in Valentinianism by his acceptance of the Old Testament. Valentinus himself, on the other hand, applied to the prophets the text of John 10:8: "All who came before me are thieves and robbers." And among the Christian intelligentsia of the second century, revulsion from the Old Testament must have been widespread. It was, to an educated Greek, an unpleasant book. Its legislation seemed trivial, and some of its morality was clearly immoral. The God who spoke to Israel was unworthy of the respect of philosophers. In such works as the *True Word* of Celsus we see common complaints against the book.[8] And yet the church had prepared no really satisfactory answer to set before critics. The penetrating intuitions of Paul and of the author of Hebrews were satisfying to the faith of those who stood within the community; but the church was eager to present its faith to those without. Some theory of the relation between the Old Testament and the New had to be formulated in order for both to be interpreted to the outside world.

It was the contribution of Irenaeus which ultimately made such a presentation possible.[9] He was a convinced believer in the importance of tradition, and traced his own spiritual ancestry back through Polycarp of Smyrna to the apostle John. In Lyons about the year 180 he composed his five books "On the Detection and Overthrow of Knowledge Falsely So-Called." In this work, directed largely against Valentinians and Marcionites, he sets forth what he regarded as simple traditional Christianity. Valentinians and Marcionites agree in assigning the Old Testament to a God inferior to the God of the New Testament. It therefore becomes necessary for Irenaeus to prove on New Testament grounds that the same God reveals himself in both Testaments. The theory which he reaches by means of his investigations into the meaning of scripture, and as a result of his instruction by teachers whom he admires and follows,[10] is that the revelation of God in the Law of the Old Testament was real and, for its day, valid; but God has now been pleased to reveal himself in a new way. Irenaeus' view of the relation of the Old Testament to the New is considerably more historical than that of any of his predecessors. As a traditionalist he does not reject other explanations of this relation; he combines the theories of others with his own.

In the course of his argument he discusses the problem of the interpretation of scripture. The Old Testament is full of types. The "treasure hidden in a field" (Matt. 13:44) is Christ hidden in the scriptures and made known through types and parables:

> For every prophecy, before it comes about, is an enigma and a contradiction to men; but when the time comes, and what was prophesied takes place, it receives a most certain exegesis. And therefore when the Law is read by Jews at the present time, it is like a myth; for they do not have the explanation of everything, which is the coming of the Son of God as man. But when it is read by Christians, it is a treasure, hidden in the field but revealed by the cross of Christ [Irenaeus, *Adv. haer.* 4.26.1].

This true exegesis was taught by the Lord himself after his resurrection (Luke 24:27). It is the method by which the Bible is to be read in the church. The method of the Valentinians, on the other hand, is compared to the destructiveness of a man who takes the mosaic portrait of a king and converts it into a picture of a dog or fox (1.8.1).

We can best discover Irenaeus' own exegetical principles by examining the charges which he brings against his opponents. He has two main criticisms to make. In the first place, his adversaries neglect the order and the context of the passages they interpret. They take isolated passages and words and interpret them in the light of their own speculative theories. For instance, in the prologue to the Gospel of John, Ptolemaeus found the various aeons of the Valentinian system, such as Father, Grace, Only Begotten, and others. Irenaeus points out that "the apostle did not speak of the unions of the aeons, but our Lord Jesus Christ" (1.9.2). Another example of the same kind of exegetical fancy he finds in the writings of students of Homer. They amuse themselves and one another by combining lines from the *Iliad* and *Odyssey*, by means of which they can tell an entirely new story. These combinations can deceive simple people; but the student of Homer will recognize that one verse is spoken about Odysseus, another about Heracles, another about Priam, and another about Menelaus and Agamemnon (1.9.4).

The second charge that he brings against the Valentinians is that they interpret the clear and obvious by the dark and obscure. Indeed, there is only one article of faith which is absolutely clear in the scriptures: there is only one God, who made everything through his Word (2.27.2). This, as it happens, is the one article they deny. And if they would interpret the scriptures properly, they would not expound their doctrines out of the most mysterious passages of parables and allegories, but from the passages which are clear. Irenaeus does not intend to deny the multiplicity of meanings in scripture or the possibility of an allegorical interpretation. He wants to avoid the explanation of one ambiguity through another ambiguity (2.10.1).

Above all for Irenaeus, who is defending the mainstream of Christian faith against able enemies, there is one standard of correct interpretation. The standard is the rule of faith as preserved in churches in the apostolic succession. Although this view was more fully developed at a later date,[11] Irenaeus is really the father of authoritative exegesis in the church. In his opinion truth is to be found only within the church. An instructive passage shows us his dislike of philosophical learning. In natural science

> many things escape our knowledge, and we entrust them to God; for he must excel over all. What if we try to set forth the cause of the rising of the Nile? We say many things, some perhaps persuasive, others perhaps not persuasive: what is true and certain and sure lies with God [2.28.2].

Such questions can never be solved. Christians, however, have the rule of faith which is also the rule of truth. If they cannot find solutions for all the questions which are asked them about the scriptures, they should leave such matters to God, for the scriptures are complete and perfect, since they were spoken by the Word of God and by his Spirit (2.28.1).

> True knowledge is the teaching of the apostles, and the ancient order of the Church in all the world, and the form of the body of Christ according to the successions of bishops, to whom they transmitted the Church which is in each place, which has come down even to us, guarded without the composition of writings by a very thorough treatment (the rule of faith), neither increased nor diminished. In it there is a reading without falsification, and a lawful and diligent exegesis of the scriptures . . . [4.33.8].

The teaching of the apostles is the true understanding of the Bible, and if anyone wishes to learn this true understanding he should read the scriptures with the presbyters of the church, with whom is the apostolic doctrine (4.32.1). All other interpretations have fallen from the truth.

In the teaching of Irenaeus the interpretation of the Bible enters a new phase. The Christian interpreter is no longer content to appeal only to his inspired intuitions, as in the case of the writers of the New Testament, or to what is self-evidently rational (as the school of Alexandria was to appeal), but to an authority which is at once external and internal. The authority of the church is external because it did not constitute the gospel; the gospel brought both the scriptures and the church into existence. And yet it is internal, for the scriptures are the church's books, and the church has been entrusted with the ministry of the gospel. And when the gospel is being interpreted as a kind of theosophy, the institutional authority of the church can play an important role. We shall examine the claims of authoritative interpretation in a later chapter.

Irenaeus was also of great significance in his analysis of the relation between the two Testaments. Indeed, he was the first Christian theologian to take biblical history seriously, and to set forth the permanent value of the Law. He is completely a man of the late second century; and yet many of his insights are like those of apostolic times. He is a bishop of the Catholic church, and since he regards the primary function of the church as the transmission of the true tradition, he must constantly appeal to the revelation contained in scripture. The work of the apologists is not lost; it is simply assimilated and corrected.

And yet the work of Irenaeus is not completely satisfying. The authority of the church has been exalted, but the liberty of the human spirit has tended to vanish. Irenaeus could not speak the language of the educated world of Alexandria. And if the Christian scriptures were not only authoritative but also rational, some other form of interpretation had to be discovered. Divine grace was not the only requirement for exegesis; further requirements were set forth by the Alexandrian school. Yet we should not suppose that the attitude of Irenaeus was contradicted by the Alexandrians. For him and for them scripture contains a great mystery. It speaks in a language of symbols. Their emphasis on the allegorical interpretation supplements Irenaeus' work. It does not supplant it.

6

The School of
Alexandria

Recent scholarship had made it a question whether we can properly speak of an exegetical "school" of Alexandria. Philo seems to
have been largely without influence in his own Jewish community;
the so-called founder of the Christian catechetical school, Pan-
taenus, is somewhat obscure. Only in the time of Origen does the
school emerge into the clear light of historical knowledge. Nevertheless, there are weighty reasons for discussing the interpretation
of scripture by the Alexandrians as a group. All of them worked in
the same city and were influenced by its atmosphere of wealth and
culture; all of them shared, to a considerable extent, the same attitude towards the difficulties of scripture. And while all of them
were subjectively loyal to the religious traditions within which
they had been brought up or to which they had been converted,
they were suspected, either by their contemporaries or by later authoritative teachers within their tradition, of aberrations from orthodoxy.

Since our theme is the Christian emergence, a brief mention of
Philo of Alexandria must suffice.[1] We shall not consider either the
very extensive copying of his writings in Clement or Origen's references to him as an exegetical forerunner. It will be enough to see
how he moved into the Greek world and thus prepared the way for
the Alexandrian Christians. The principal difference between the
exegesis of Philo and that of his rabbinic contemporaries is not so
much in the systematic method which he employs as in the underlying principle in his work which is not found in theirs. From the
Stoics Philo had learned to divide allegorization into two classes,
the "physical" and the "ethical." In the first classification he could
place interpretations of scripture which referred to God and the nature of the world; in the second, interpretations which referred to

the duties of man. For example, he and his predecessors agree that the seven-branched candelabrum really means the seven planets (physical allegory), and that Abraham and Sarah stand for Mind and Virtue (ethical).[2]

The necessity of allegorization he finds demonstrated by scripture itself:

> We must turn to allegory, the method dear to men with their eyes opened. Indeed the sacred oracles most evidently afford us the clues for the use of this method. For they say that in the garden (of Eden) there are trees in no way resembling those with which we are familiar, but trees of Life, of Immortality, of Knowledge, of Apprehension, of Understanding, of the conception of good and evil [*Plant.* 36].

Certain principles guide us in its application. In the first place, there are certain situations in which the literal sense of a passage must be denied. In the most common instance of this denial, passages containing anything unworthy of God must be interpreted allegorically; but it applies also to passages which are difficult to understand, whether they seem historically improbable or contain inconsistencies. After the literal sense has been excluded, the allegorical sense or senses can be introduced. In general it is obvious that any writing can be understood in several ways; and this Philo regards as a justification for his doctrine of a multiplicity of meanings. If something is stated which seems perfectly obvious, there must be a deeper meaning hidden within the statement. And since to Philo as to every Jew of his time the scriptures are the work of God, every expression, every word, and every letter has its meaning. Like the Stoics he discovers this hidden meaning by etymology, often highly forced, and arithmology. The meaning of a word can be discovered in its source, and numbers have special significance.[3]

What does Philo endeavor to prove by means of this exegetical method? His fundamental theory is apologetic. In his mind many of the insights of Judaism, properly understood, do not differ from the highest insights of Greek philosophy. God revealed himself to the chosen people of Israel, but he revealed himself in no radically different way from the way in which he revealed himself to the

Greeks. And therefore Philo finds it necessary to explain away the apparent anthropomorphism of God and the apparent exclusiveness of Israel in favor of a philosopher's God and a Hellenistic man's internationalism.

The most militant allegorizers of the second century were the Gnostics, men who generally maintained a thoroughgoing cosmic dualism and believed that the God who like them regarded the created world as a tragic mistake had given his revelation through Jesus only to them. They alone could understand the mysterious parables and enigmatic sayings in the gospels and other Christian documents, for they alone were "spiritual" beings. Taking New Testament passages with the severest literalism, they then proceeded to claim that their meaning could be understood only in the light of the Gnostic myths about the spiritual world, man's fallen state, and the redemption of the "divine spark." This is to say that they separated Jesus from the church and removed his sayings from the contexts which the evangelists had supplied, to some extent anticipating the work of more recent critics.[4]

Such conscious neglect of contexts is characteristic of Gnostics both Jewish and Christian. For example, the Old Testament was compiled and transmitted by those who believed in the unity of God. They regarded Yahweh as the same God as Elohim or El-Shaddai or Yahweh Sabaoth. Gnostic readers, on the contrary, denied the unity of God, and held that these names referred to various deities subordinate to the true, unknown Father. Similarly they regarded the Father of Jesus as quite different from the malevolent Creator God whose emotions and actions are portrayed in the Old Testament. Denying the unity of God, they also denied the unity of the church and regarded themselves as superior to the ordinary Christians who were animated by soul but not by divine spirit.

Such arguments adversely affected more orthodox Christians because the Gnostics were the first, it would appear, to provide relatively systematic exegesis of the New Testament. The Valentinian Ptolemaeus, as we have seen, wrote not only on the Decalogue; he also wrote on the prologue to John. Another Valentinian, Heracleon, produced the first commentary to be written on one of the gospels.[5] This commentary exists today only in fragments preserved by Origen in his *Commentary on the Gospel of John*, but from these fragments we can see how fanciful Heracleon's allego-

rization (like Origen's) was. While occasionally he is sober and
sensible, most of his interpretations reject the literal meaning of
the stories in the Fourth Gospel in order to find hidden symbolism.
Everything which Jesus says and does has a timeless meaning
which has been revealed to Valentinians. If we possessed the introduction to his commentary we might know how Heracleon justified his position. We know that Valentinus claimed to have been
the disciple of Theodas, a companion of Paul (Clement, *Str.*
7.106.4); presumably Heracleon derived his knowledge from him
and interpreted the gospel in its light.

It was Clement of Alexandria, however, who first among Christians undertook to justify and explain the meaning of the allegorical method. And yet his thought is hardly ever systematic. He is
not attempting to construct a theological system in the light of his
interpretation of scripture, but simply to use scripture to illustrate
his already formed thought. He had apparently come to Christianity through teaching which he accepted without much question.
And when he tries to find this teaching expressed in the words of
scripture he begins to develop a theory of the symbolism of the Bible. He believes that all scripture speaks in a mysterious language
of symbols (*Str.* 6.124.6), just as all those, barbarians and Greeks,
who have discussed theology have veiled the ultimate reasons
of things; they have transmitted the truth only through enigmas
and symbols, allegories, metaphors, and analogous figures (*Str.*
5.21.4). Moses, Plato, and the Egyptians who used hieroglyphics
spoke in the same way.

When Clement comes to the interpretation of scripture we find
that in practice his exegesis is based on that of Philo. Every word
and syllable of scripture has its meaning, but, since it is written
symbolically, the meaning is usually not the obvious one. Mondésert has suggested that there are five possible senses in which
Clement might interpret the words of his text:[6] (1) the historical
sense, in which he usually takes the stories of biblical history; (2)
the doctrinal sense, moral, religious, and theological, according to
which biblical statements are taken directly into his own theological thought. These first two methods do not go far beyond literalism, although the atmosphere of Clement's thought prevents them
from being matter-of-fact. (3) The prophetic sense includes both
genuine prophecies and "types" which according to Christian tradi-

tion Clement found in the Old Testament. (4) A philosophical sense, which owes much to the Stoics and to Philo, includes both 'cosmic' and 'psychological' meanings of scripture. For example, the tables of the Law symbolize the universe; Sarah and Hagar symbolize true wisdom and pagan philosophy. (5) And finally there is a mystical sense, according to which for instance Lot's wife symbolizes the attachment to earthly things, to impiety and to the impious, which produces in the soul a kind of blindness in regard to God and to his truth (*Protr.* 103.4, 1, 74 St.; 159 Mondésert). Not all these senses are distinct: indeed, Clement is quite capable of taking a text in two or three ways at the same time. But any of them can be found in any text of scripture.

These are the senses in which scripture can be taken, according to Clement. How is the reader to choose among them? What guiding principle is to govern his or her interpretation? For one who was devoted to the church there could be only one answer: Faith in Christ, in his person and in his work, is the key to scripture.[7] The Logos who spoke in the Old Testament finally revealed himself in the New, and the Christian is able to understand all scripture in the light of the knowledge which Christ has given. By such understanding he or she will eventually come to the true *gnosis* which contains the higher truths of the religion, and will become a Gnostic.

In Clement we find the allegorical method of Philo baptized into Christ. Like his forerunners in Christianity, Clement makes use of a Christocentric interpretation of the scriptures, especially the Old Testament. His results are more varied than theirs because he has broader interests. He comes from a higher intellectual atmosphere than they, and what his treatment of scripture lacks in piety— though he is always a devout Christian—it gains in breadth of human and intellectual interest. Nevertheless he is not a great theologian. He does not possess the intellectual rigour which produces theological systems. His mind is not sufficiently precise and his interest in any one subject is not sufficiently intense for him to produce a thoroughgoing dogmatic work. This task was reserved for Origen, in his *De Principiis.*

Origen is the most distinguished member of the Alexandrian school, and it is he who sets forth most thoroughly and adequately the principles of Christian allegorization.[8] He was the first Alexandrian to teach theology under the auspices of the church. The fourth book of his *De Principiis* deals with the inspiration and interpretation of scripture. At the beginning he undertakes to prove briefly the fact of the inspiration of scripture. There are two points to be made: (1) the success of the Christian movement, which Jesus predicted, shows its superhuman nature; and (2) "after the advent of Jesus the inspiration of the prophetic words and the spiritual nature of Moses' law came to light." The fulfillment of prophecy is the proof of its inspiration. At this point Origen turns to the question of the interpretation of scripture. The fundamental principle underlying Origen's argument is this:

> Because the principal aim was to announce the connection that exists among spiritual events, those that have already happened and those that are yet to come to pass, whenever the Word found that things which had happened in history could be harmonized with these mystical events he used them, concealing from the multitude their deeper meaning. But wherever in the narrative the accomplishment of some particular deeds, which had been previously recorded for the sake of their more mystical meanings, did not correspond with the sequence of the intellectual truths, the scripture wove into the story something which did not happen, occasionally something which could not happen, and occasionally something which might have happened but in fact did not [*De Pr.* 4.2.9].

The purpose of scripture is the revelation of "intellectual truths" rather than of God's working in history. Sometimes, indeed, the "history" merely conceals the truths. The principle applies to both Testaments.

The examples which he gives in support of this principle make most interesting reading. In the Old Testament Origen finds incredible the picture of the first three "days" of creation without sun, moon, and stars; the "farming" activity of God in "planting" a garden; the concept of a literal tree of "good and evil"; God's "walking" in the garden; and Cain's "going out" from the "face" of God. There are "thousands" of such instances.

> Even the gospels are full of passages of this kind, as when the devil takes Jesus up into a high mountain in order to show him from thence the kingdoms of the whole world and the glory of them (Matt. 4:8). For what man who does not read such passages care-

fully would fail to condemn those who believe that with the eye of
the flesh, which requires a great height to enable us to perceive what
is below and at our feet, the kingdoms of the Persians, Scythians,
Indians and Parthians were seen, and the manner in which their rul-
ers are glorified by men? And the careful reader will detect thousands of other passages in the gospels like this, which will convince
him that events which did not take place at all are woven into the records of what literally did happen [*De Pr.* 4.3.1.].

Moreover, much of the legislation in both Testaments cannot be
literally observed. Elsewhere Origen is strongly impressed with the
discrepancies between the gospels, and says that historical exegesis of them is impossible; the student will have to rely arbitrarily
on one of them, not venturing to reject wholly the belief concerning our Lord, or else accept the four and say that their truth is not
in the material letter (*In Ev. Ioh.* 10.3). Here, however, he is careful to state that some things in scripture do have a literal meaning;
"the passages which are historically true far outnumber those [his-
torically untrue] which are composed with purely spiritual meanings" (*De Pr.* 4.3.4.). But among his examples he gives none from
the New Testament, except of commandments of Jesus which are
to be obeyed.

At the conclusion of his discussion of impossibilities Origen
provides his readers with some detailed advice on the interpretation of scripture. What is to be done in the case of difficult and
ambiguous passages?

> The exact reader will hesitate in regard to some passages, finding
> himself unable to decide without considerable investigation whether
> a particular incident, believed to be history, actually happened or
> not. Accordingly he who reads in an exact manner must, in obedi-
> ence to the Savior's precept which says, "Search the scriptures"
> [John 5:39], carefully investigate how far the literal meaning is true
> and how far it is impossible, and to the utmost of his power must
> trace out from the use of similar expressions the meaning scattered
> everywhere throughout the scriptures of that which when taken liter-
> ally is impossible [*De Pr.* 4.3.5.].

All scripture has a spiritual meaning; not all has a literal meaning.
And in any event, complete understanding of the mysteries of
scripture is impossible. When St. Paul cries out, "How unsearch-

able are his judgments and his ways are past finding out" (Rom. 11:33), he does not say that his ways are hard to search out, but that they cannot be searched out at all.

> For however far one may advance in the search and make progress through an increasingly earnest study, even when aided and enlightened in mind by God's grace,he will never be able to reach the final goal of his inquiries [*De Pr.* 4.3.14.].

In his entire treatment of the allegorical method Origen is concerned to stress the ultimate mystery contained in scripture. The Bible speaks to us only in a language of symbols. And its interpretation requires a gift of divine grace. Scripture itself reveals that it is to be understood in a multiplicity of senses, for according to the Septuagint, the Greek version of the Old Testament which all the Greek fathers used, Proverbs 22:20f. reads as follows:

> Do thou portray them *threefold* in counsel and knowledge, that thou mayst answer words of truth to those who question thee [*De Pr.* 4.2.4.].

Origen interprets this passage in the light of Paul's threefold analysis of human personality (1 Thess. 5:23) into "spirit, soul, and body," and concludes that there is a "bodily" or literal sense, a "soul" or moral sense, and a "spiritual" or allegorical-mystical sense in scripture. In actual practice, however, Origen rarely makes use of the moral sense as distinct from the other two senses, and he ordinarily distinguishes merely between the "letter" and the "spirit" (2 Cor. 3:6).[9]

Why is Origen so eager to exclude the literal meaning of scripture? We must remember that there is a difference between his understanding of the literal meaning and ours. What he means by "literal" is the interpretation placed on scripture by the simplest of simple believers, those who cannot understand the meaning of metaphors, parables, or allegories, and who insist that every detail in them is literally true. Such people invariably understand poetry as prose. They believe, for example, in the literal reality of the heavenly Jerusalem described in the Apocalypse of John. Origen's interpretations are in part polemic against them. They would not be able to understand a literary analysis of figurative language, and Origen is compelled to insist on figures hidden behind every verse, indeed every word and syllable, of scripture. We can see that his method is not altogether satisfactory; it could lead to dangerous excesses; but for its time it was invaluable.

How is the interpreter to be sure that his or her exegesis is correct? We should expect to find Origen more hesitant, less certain of the accuracy of his daring allegorical interpretations than he actually is. And it is worth observing that, according to Zöllig, there are no examples in his writings where he states that his interpretation is absolutely certain.[10] Nevertheless, he knows that the exegete must pray for guidance from God, and he must work diligently as best he can. Origen also gives several practical suggestions. Paul teaches us to collect and compare one spiritual truth with others (1 Cor. 2:3); we must observe the use of words; we should compare similar texts when one is (apparently) literal and the others spiritual; and we must be guided by the rule of faith.[11] But without the allegorical method we are likely to make many mistakes.

While Origen constantly tries to express what he regards as the orthodox Christian faith, the philosophical aids to faith with which he is so much occupied tend to alter the content of that faith. We may suppose that unlike Irenaeus and other fathers of the western church Origen is not eager to apply the rule of faith as an exegetical norm. He relies far more on individual scholarship and intelligence than on any consensus of opinion. Like other Alexandrians, he is a somewhat self-conscious intellectual. For this reason it was difficult for the church to accept wholeheartedly all the implications of his theory of allegory.

His influence on later exegesis was very great. While he was bitterly attacked not only by the exegetical school of Antioch but also by such men as Jerome and Augustine, his own pupils continued his work, and even those who attacked him most vigorously were often influenced by his thought. Jerome is an example of this ambivalent attitude; at first a strong Origenist, he later became Origen's fiercest opponent. Origen's influence on medieval allegorists though indirect is incalculable. For the earlier Greek church some of the most important of his writings on exegetical subjects were collected by Basil the Great and Gregory of Nazianzus under the title *Philocalia*.

How is the school of Alexandria, with Origen its most illustrious representative, related to the general history of interpretation? Harnack scornfully dismissed Origen's work with the epithet "biblical alchemy"; and there have been many students of the fathers who agreed with him. It may also be said that his method is not as rational as we might desire, or as he thought it was. His classifications are not really convincing, and his "spiritual" interpretations are highly subjective. But we can admit today that objectivity in the interpretation of any work of the human spirit is an elusive aim; the interpreter always reads something of his own thought into what he interprets, and it is well for him if his own personality be as nearly Christian as Origen's was. Moreover, we must consider the circumstances under which Origen wrote. The Christocentric typology of St. Paul was no longer a practicable method of interpretation in the city of Alexandria. Celsus had already attacked the immorality and triviality of the scriptures, and Porphyry was soon to do so. Christians were eager to be intellectually respectable; and most philosophical schools accepted the allegorical method. The results of Origen's teaching were highly satisfactory:

> A great many heretics, and not a few of the most distinguished philosophers, studied under him diligently, receiving instruction from him not only in divine things, but also in secular philosophy. For when he perceived that any persons had superior intelligence he instructed them also in philosophic branches—in geometry, arithmetic, and other preparatory studies—and then advanced to the systems of the philosophers and explained their writings. And he made observations and comments upon each of them, so that he became celebrated as a great philosopher even among the Greeks themselves. And he instructed many of the less learned in elementary subjects (*encyclia*), saying that these would be no small help to them in the study and understanding of the divine scriptures. On this account he considered it especially necessary for himself to be skilled in secular and philosophic learning [Eusebius, *Hist. eccl.* 6.18.2ff., McGiffert].

In this description of Origen's work at Alexandria we see a whole program of Christian education. It is an answer to Celsus's charge that Christians do not wish to give or to receive a reason for their belief, that they keep repeating "Do not examine, but believe" (Origen, *Con. Cels.* 1.9). Origen, like other Christians of his time, distinguishes between the wisdom of the world and true wisdom; he also claims that the Christian is not to be a fool but to be a fool towards the wisdom of the world. "It is of much more importance to give our assent to doctrines upon grounds of reason and wisdom than on that of simple faith" (ibid., 1.13).

The allegorical method, at a critical moment in Christian history, made it possible to uphold the rationality of Christian faith. It was used to prevent obscurantism. And though we may question not only its assumptions but also its results, we must not forget what we owe to it. We are not indebted so much to the method itself as to the spirit of those who employed it. The method alone is lifeless; the spirit of the interpreter makes the text live.

7

The School of
Antioch

The allegorical method encountered considerable opposition within the church. Marcion of Pontus, as we have seen, rejected the method. Early in the third century an Egyptian bishop named Nepos wrote a *Refutation of the Allegorists*. Under the influence of his Jewish teachers Jerome turned from allegorization to an increasing respect for the literal meaning of scripture.[1] And it is likely that wherever the influence of the synagogue was felt by the church the interpretation of scripture had a tendency toward literalism.

Such was certainly the case at Antioch. For centuries the Jewish community there was prominent and influential. The earliest Antiochene exegesis which we possess, an interpretation of Genesis by Theophilus of Antioch, is largely derived from Jewish teachers. In the third century it was said that the rigorous monotheism of Paul of Samosata was due to his association with Judaism. The Antiochene text of the Greek Old Testament often ascribed to Lucian seems to be the same as that used earlier by Josephus, and presumably was current among Jews. A little later we find Dorotheus, head of the catechetical school at Antioch, studying Hebrew. And some of the interpretations of Theodore of Mopsuestia are criticized by his disciple Theodoret as being Jewish rather than Christian.[2] Naturally these interpreters rejected all allegorization.

Dorotheus, as the church historian Eusebius tells us, interpreted the scriptures "with moderation"; that is to say, he did not allegorize them. Eustathius, who was bishop of Antioch, wrote a treatise on the Witch of Endor against Origen, who strangely enough had taken this story literally. Eustathius attacks Origen both for his literalism here and for his ordinary allegorization. Another adherent of the school, Diodorus of Tarsus, composed a book called *What is the Difference Between Theory and Allegory.* "Theory," as we shall see, is the true meaning of the text as the Antiochenes understand it. Finally Theodore of Mopsuestia himself wrote *Concerning Allegory and History Against Origen.* The differences between the schools of Antioch and Alexandria were not slight, and the Antiochenes were vigorous defenders of their own view.

The Alexandrines, naturally, appealed to the use of allegorization by the apostle Paul in the fourth chapter of Galatians. The Antiochenes, on the other hand, explained that while he uses the word he does not really interpret allegorically. There is a great difference, they say, between what the apostle means and what the Alexandrines mean. The apostle believes in the reality of the events which he describes, and uses them for examples. The Alexandrines, on the other hand, deprive the whole biblical history of its reality. Adam was not really Adam, paradise was not really paradise, the serpent was not a real serpent. In that case, Theodore asks, since there are no real events, since Adam was not really disobedient, how did death enter the world, and what meaning does our salvation have? The apostle must have believed in the reality of the events he describes, for in Romans 5:18f. he refers to the disobedience of Adam, and in 2 Corinthians 11:3 to the serpent's seduction of Eve.[3]

The twelfth chapter of Isho'dad's *Introduction to the Psalms* comes from the ninth century but it is largely based on the exegetical theory of Theodore, and clearly sets forth his objections to the theory of Origen:

> People ask what the difference is between allegorical exegesis and historical exegesis. We reply that it is great and not small; just as the first leads to impiety, blasphemy and falsehood, so the other is conformed to truth and faith. It was the impious Origen of Alexandria who invented this art of allegory. Just as poets and geometricians, when they wish to raise their disciples from material and visible things to things hidden and invisible, erring in regard to the eternity of incorporeal matter and to indivisible atoms, say: "Just as it is not these visible signs which are signs for reading, but their hidden meanings, so from created natures one must rise by the image of thought to their eternal nature"; just so, Origen taught. . . . The Psalms and the Prophets who spoke of the captivity and the return of

the people, he explained as teaching the captivity of the soul far from truth and its return to the faith. . . . They do not interpret paradise as it is, or Adam, or Eve, or any existing thing.[4]

After setting forth the nature of Origen's exegesis, Isho'dad proceeds to refute it.

One example will suffice to show the nature of the others. When the apostle writes: "This rock was Christ" [1 Cor. 10:4], he clearly shows, they say, that even while appearing to be a rock, in reality this rock was Christ, secretly working for the salvation of those who are like him. Similarly in regard to Melchizedek, they claim that he was the Son of God. For according to them our Savior did not appear once in this world, but many times; he has revealed himself to the various ages according to their capacity, and he has been with all of them. He even had to come for inanimate rocks, in order to deliver those who were held by them.

Those stupid people have not observed that the apostles in citing the words of the Old Testament do not cite them in only one way; sometimes they cite them to show their fulfilment, at other times as examples for the exhortation and correction of their hearers, or else to confirm the teaching of the faith, even though according to the historical circumstances these words were set forth for other purposes. Now when our Lord applies Psalms 8 and 110 to himself, and when Peter in the Acts and Paul in his epistles apply to our Lord the same psalms as well as Psalms 2 and 45, they take them in their true sense. But when our Lord says on the cross, "My God, my God, why hast thou forsaken me?" [Psalm 22:2] . . . etc., these words are said by a comparison according to the resemblance of the events, although in their context their application is different. Now the difference between these things is clear from the context for those who wish to know the truth.[5]

When Paul cites scripture, therefore, he does so for the sake of comparison. This is the customary usage of the New Testament. For example, Moses lifted up the serpent in the desert. This figure is applied by Jesus to himself (John 3:14). If Jesus himself had been the serpent, how could he have compared himself to it?

When Paul says that all these things took place for an example [1 Cor. 10:11], he does not affirm that they were without value for those to whom they happened, those who are named, or that everything was done for us.[6]

The school of Antioch insisted on the historical reality of the biblical revelation. They were unwilling to lose it in a world of symbols and shadows. They were more Aristotelian than Platonist. Where the Alexandrines use the word *theory* as equivalent to allegorical interpretation, the Antiochene exegetes use it for a sense of scripture higher or deeper than the literal or historical meaning, but firmly based on the letter.[7] This understanding does not deny the literal meaning of scripture but is grounded on it, as an image is based on the thing represented and points towards it. Both image and thing are comprehensible at the same time. There is no hidden meaning which only a Gnostic can comprehend. John Chrysostom observes that "everywhere in scripture there is this law, that when it allegorizes, it also gives the explanation of the allegory."[8]

The meaning of *theory* is most clearly evident in the Antiochene understanding of the prophets. The Antiochene writers rejected the Alexandrian opinion that the reference of the prophets to the coming of Christ was something added to the original prophecy, that it was an allegorical understanding. In their view the prophet himself foresaw both the immediate event which was to come in the history of ancient Israel, and the ultimate coming of Christ. The prophet's prediction was at the same time both historical and Christocentric. It contains a double sense, historical and messianic. This double sense is not something which allegorists superimpose upon an originally literal meaning.[9]

Theodore of Mopsuestia, the greatest interpreter of the School of Antioch, was also the most individualistic; and in his work we find a distinction made between those prophecies which are genuinely messianic and those which are entirely historical. Four psalms really refer to Christ: these are Psalms 2, 8, 45, and 110. Such psalms as the twenty-second, on the other hand, have an original historical meaning, and can be understood only typically of Christ. When Theodore's opponents pointed out that in the Septuagint, the Greek Old Testament, the Twenty-Second Psalm was entitled, "At the end," and thus clearly pointed toward Christ, he explained to them that the titles of many psalms are not authentic.[10] Many other prophecies in the Old Testament, he held, have no messianic reference.

But what shall we say of the books of Old and New Testament

alike which contain no prophetic elements, either messianic or historical? They are books which contain merely human wisdom, and according to Theodore they are to be excluded from the canon of scripture. They are not inspired by the Holy Spirit. The book of Job, for example, was written after the exile by a poet acquainted with Greek learning. We know he was a poet because he composed discourses in the name of Job and his friends and even in the name of God; these discourses bear no relation to reality. He was acquainted with Greek learning because, according to the Septuagint, the third daughter of Job is called "horn of Amalthea" (Job 42:14). Unfortunately for this argument, the girl's name is simply a mistranslation of *qerenhappuk*, "horn for paint," a cosmetic accessory. But Theodore was convinced that the wisdom literature reflects a wisdom merely human and that it cannot be included in the canon of inspired scripture. Some of the historical books, such as Chronicles and Ezra-Nehemiah, are merely historical and are therefore to be rejected.[11]

Theodore's analysis of the Song of Songs is interesting. He points out that there is no mention of God in it, and that it is read publicly neither by Jews nor by Christians. It may properly be compared with the *Symposium* of Plato. Its historical occasion is the wedding of Solomon with the daughter of Pharaoh. At this point in his discussion a certain sense of decorum overcomes Theodore, and he insists that the wedding took place not for pleasure, but for the political stability of Israel. Moreover, since the princess was black and therefore not especially attractive to the court of Solomon, he built a palace for her and composed this song—so that she would not be irritated and so that enmity would not arise between him and Pharaoh![12]

In dealing with the New Testament, Theodore followed the tradition of the orient and refused to admit the Catholic epistles to his canon of scripture. He also rejected the epistle of James, possibly because of its reference to Job (James 5:11), more probably because of its similarity to the wisdom literature of the Old Testament.[13] His *Commentary on the Gospel of John* reflects his customary interest in the work of the Holy Spirit. He knew that in the Acts of the Apostles the Holy Spirit is not given the apostles until Pentecost; indeed, it is not even promised them until later than the

time described in John 20:22f. Theodore therefore held that the
apostles never confessed the divinity of Christ during his earthly
life, since they had not received the Spirit. They received this faith
at Pentecost. The title "Son of God" means no more than "Messiah." And even after Jesus' resurrection the apostles did not call
him divine. When Thomas exclaims, "My Lord and my God" (John
20:28), this is simply an exclamation in praise of God for the miracle which he has seen.[14]

The exegetical work of Theodore was ordered to be burned by
the Second Council of Constantinople in 553. Not only was he
considered responsible for the Christological errors of his pupil
Nestorius, but also he had denied the inspiration of some of the
books which the church had judged canonical. But the influence of
the school of Antioch, and of Theodore himself, did not come to
an end. It reached the later church not only through two famous
commentators but also through two widely used handbooks of
interpretation.

In the first place, John Chrysostom, archbishop of Constantinople, was like Theodore a pupil of Diodorus of Tarsus; he continued to make use of his master's literalist method in his sermons
and commentaries. While Chrysostom does not rigidly exclude allegorization, he usually restricts himself to typology. Indeed, he
criticizes Paul's use of language in Galatians 4:24:

> By a misuse of language he called the type allegory. What he means
> is this: the history itself not only has the apparent meaning but also
> proclaims other matters; therefore it is called allegory. But what did
> it proclaim? Nothing other than everything that now is.[15]

Here Chrysostom reflects the Antiochene concept of *theory*. Elsewhere he explains the relation of the two meanings of scripture by
a parallel from art:

> The type is given the name of the truth until the truth is about to
> come; but when the truth has come, the name is no longer used.
> Similarly in painting: an artist sketches a king, but until the colours
> are applied he is not called a king; and when they are put on the type
> is hidden by the truth and is not visible; and then we say, "Behold
> the king."[16]

The historical meaning is the outline; but the final form of the por-

trait is found only in the typological meaning. Chrysostom's interpretations of scripture were highly influential upon later interpreters. They often constitute the main source for catenas, chains of
exegetical materials. Thomas Aquinas greatly admired his work.

Not only through Chrysostom, however, but also through a far
more learned exegete, "the greatest doctor of the church in ex-
pounding the sacred scriptures," did this influence come down.
This doctor was Jerome. He was by no means so extreme a literalist as Theodore of Mopsuestia. He stood closer to such a writer as
Chrysostom. But the main lines of his exegesis moved further and
further away from the allegorization which he originally admired.
He came to emphasize the historical reality of the Old Testament
narratives and prophecies. In part this emphasis was due to his textual studies[17] and to his growing knowledge of Jewish exegesis; in
part it was due to the school of Antioch which shared precisely
these interests. It might almost be said that the school of Antioch
was responsible for the production of the Vulgate. It will be re-
called, on the other hand, that Theodore of Mopsuestia like Augustine regretted Jerome's deviations from the inspired Greek version.[18]

Jerome's first commentary was a pure allegorization. At Antioch, however, he came under the influence of the literal-historical method, taught him by Apollinaris of Laodicea. Thereafter he
was unable to feel the attraction of the allegorical method, even as
presented by Gregory of Nazianzus, the great Origenist. No matter
how ingenious the allegorization, Jerome had to insist upon the reality of the literal meaning. The deeper meaning of scripture was
built on the literal, not opposed to it. Everything written in scripture took place and at the same time has a meaning more than historical. This meaning is based on the *Hebraica veritas*, the truth
expressed in Hebrew. We must have a *spiritualis intelligentia*, a
spiritual understanding of scripture, wh:ch goes beyond the
carneus sensus (the fleshly sense) but will not be opposed to it.
Through Jerome, then, in the second place, Antiochene literalism
was mediated to the later church.[19]

The influence of the school of Antioch was also felt more directly. Two handbooks of interpretation are still extant which express the Antiochene attitude. The earlier of the two is the *Intro-*

duction to the Divine Scriptures of Adrian apparently written about 425.[20] It consists largely of an explanation of the meaning of Hebrew idioms and of biblical phraseology. Anthropomorphisms, for instance, do not need to be taken literally, but refer to various attributes of God. At the end of the work Adrian points out that there are two forms of writing in the scriptures, prophetic and historical. Each has its own purpose. And for the interpretation of each, literalism is primary. But the interpreter must not be content to remain in literalism; he must go on to deeper understanding, based on the literal meaning. In conclusion he distinguishes between poetry and prose and briefly discusses poetical meters.[21] Few "introductions" to scripture have been more sensible than this.

The other manual of interpretation is the *Regulative Institutes of the Divine Law* by Junilius Africanus, based on the teaching of "Paul the Persian," and composed about 550. The Nestorian school of Edessa in Syria had preserved the teaching of Theodore, and when in 489 the emperor Zeno proscribed Nestorianism the school fled to Nisibis in Persia; there they preserved Antiochene exegesis. "Paul the Persian" was probably metropolitan of Nisbis.[22] From the East the teaching of Theodore returned to the West. Junilius's work was popular; soon after its publication Cassiodorus recommended it, and in the Carolingian renaissance of learning there were copies to be found in at least five monastic libraries.[23]

In Syria and at Nisibis the Nestorians had studied the hermeneutical work of Aristotle, and had systematized Theodore's typology along Aristotelian lines. At times this systematization seems rather excessive. For example, Junilius classifies the types of scripture in four groups: *Grata gratis, maesta maestis, maestis grata, gratis maesta* (2.17, 510f. Kihn). Christ's resurrection is a joyful type of our future joyful rising (Col. 3:3f.); Satan's sad fall was a type of our sad fall (2 Pet. 2:4ff.); Adam's sad fall was a type of our Savior's joyful righteousness (Rom. 5:19); and joyful baptism is a type of the Lord's sad death (Rom. 6:3). It is plain that the typology of the New Testament is not really so simple as this; and the fourth classification seems to lie outside the range of typology.

Junilius distinguishes prophecy from type in this way:

In prophecy future events are signified by words, insofar as there are words available, but in types events are declared by events; in definition we can combine these two elements and say that prophecy is a type in words, insofar as words are available, and on the other hand the type is a prophecy in events, insofar as the events are known as events [2.16, 509].

The interpretation of scripture, however, goes beyond any grammatical analysis, and must be more deeply defined. It is based on historical meanings, but is not limited to them:

What should we keep in mind for the understanding of the scriptures? What is said must be suited to him who says it, it must not disagree with the causes for which it is said, and it must agree with the times, places, order of events, and intention of scripture. What do we say is the intention of scripture? What the Lord himself said, that we should love God with all our heart and soul and our neighbors as ourselves [2.28, 526].

Here we see the influence of Augustine's *De doctrina christiana* (see pp. 78ff.), and the intrusion of a principle which Augustine used to justify allegorization. Another statement of Junilius would not have displeased Origen. In discussing the relation of faith to reason he says:

What reason teaches, faith understands, and where reason is lacking, faith leads the way. For we do not believe whatever we hear, but what reason does not disprove [2.30, 528].

Junilius, however, does not intend to use this principle for allegorization. He wishes to employ it in defense of Theodore's limitation of the messianic texts in the Old Testament. And when he asks how many messianic texts there are, we are not surprised to find the number set forth by Theodore (2.22, 518). Unlike Theodore, Junilius does not venture to reject books from the canon of scripture. But he sets up three classes of books, those of perfect authority, those of moderate authority, and those of none. The last group consists of the apocryphal books rejected by all; the second group consists of the books which Theodore rejected and which "many people add"; only the first group, unquestioned by Theodore, is completely satisfactory.[24]

The canon of Theodore and Junilius was not destined for permanent survival, although Martin Luther was to endeavor to exclude certain books from the list of scripture. But the literal-historical exegetical method of the Antiochenes was strongly influential upon the thought of later Christianity. It is reflected in medieval interest in Jewish exegesis and in the interpretation of Thomas Aquinas; it became a pillar of the Reformation. Modern historical interpreters have praised Theodore for his boldness; but he is not an historical critic, and he turns his back on some of the intuitional typology of the New Testament. Nevertheless, in the long run the literal historical method became the principal exegetical method of the Christian church.

8

The Authoritative
Interpretation

The uneasiness of Christian exegetes in their conflicts with Marcion and the Valentinians did not diminish. Later minority groups continued to appeal to the authority of scripture, and often seemed to prove their case. Interpreters within the mainstream of tradition might accuse those outside of distorting the plain meaning of the text, but as allegorization came to be employed by orthodox theologians this charge lost much of its force. Tertullian, indeed, goes so far as to say that the appeal to scripture ought not to be made, since the assurance of victory was very slight (*Praesc*. 19). And at a later date such heresiarchs as Arius actually seemed to have as many texts of scripture on their side as orthodox writers did. Moreover there were conflicts within the church between the school of Alexandria and the school of Antioch. Such a theologian as Methodius believed that his interpretations were made "according to the mind of the scriptures";[1] but most orthodox writers were not so confident. They felt the need of an external authority which would permanently fix the meaning of scripture.

Such an authority was the Catholic church. Here the scriptures had been preserved by those who stood in the apostolic succession; here they had been properly interpreted according to the oral tradition which had come down from the apostles and had been formulated in the rule of faith. Irenaeus, as we have seen, sets forth this theory in his work against heresies:

> Since we have as a rule the truth itself and a clear testimony concerning God, we must not fall away into one solution after another of our questions, and reject our firm and reliable knowledge of God [*Adv. haer*. ii.28.1].

By means of this rule, handed down only in the apostolic succession, we can obtain exposition "without peril," "legitimate exposition." The Valentinians might claim that their succession too comes down from the apostles; but its historicity is uncertain. Our list is preserved at Rome and in Asia Minor, complete with every link intact.

It is obvious that such a principle of interpretation possesses great advantages. For those who stand within the church it is natural to seek the church's mind in interpreting her books, the scriptures. And in a relatively early period of ecclesiastical history, when on the one hand the church's faith had not greatly developed from that of apostolic times, and on the other there was fairly general agreement as to the meaning of scripture, the principle of interpretation according to the rule of faith had an attractive simplicity. Orthodox interpreters were largely united against Marcion and the Valentinians. The possibility of radical disagreement seemed fairly remote.

Moreover, it could be claimed that Paul had implied such a principle of interpretation. The thoroughgoing traditionalism of the pastoral epistles pointed the way towards the outlook of Irenaeus; and such an expression as that used in 1 Timothy 1:8, to the effect that the Law must be used "lawfully," would suggest the possibility of "lawful" interpretation. But Irenaeus merely hints at the idea of "legitimate" as opposed to "illegitimate" interpretation. He does not make use of the language of law.

The development of the argument from the church's possession of the scriptures is made by Tertullian of Carthage, early in the third century. It is possible, but by no means certain, that Tertullian was himself a lawyer; in any event he must have studied Roman law with intense interest. And in his *De praescriptione haereticorum*, written about the year 200, he sets forth the arguments by means of which heretics are to be kept from utilizing the church's book. Tertullian was an admirer of Irenaeus, and owed much of his understanding of Christianity to him; we are not surprised, therefore, to find him developing and extending an argument which Irenaeus had earlier undertaken. The most important part of the *De praescriptione* for us is its central section, in which, after simple pastoral advice to simple readers, Tertullian sets forth the argument from law. At the beginning of this section he describes the purpose of his brief:

They put forward the scriptures and by their audacity make an immediate impression on some people. In the struggle itself they wear out the strong, seduce the weak; as they depart they leave a scruple in the heart of the mediocre ones. Therefore it is here above all that we bar their way by declaring them inadmissible to any dispute over the scriptures. If their strength consists in the fact that they are able to possess them, we must see to whom the scriptures belong, so that no one is admitted to them who is not legally competent.[2]

The answer to this question does not take long to set forth. The scriptures belong to the church:

For there where it will appear that the truth of Christian discipline and faith are found, there also will be the true scriptures, the true interpretations, and all the true Christian traditions.[3]

This analysis rests upon three fundamental assumptions. In the first place, Jesus Christ came to preach the truth of revelation; next he entrusted this truth to the apostles; and finally, the apostles transmitted it to the apostolic churches which they founded. Therefore only the churches which stand in the succession of the apostles possess the teaching of Christ (*Pr.* 20f.). Tertullian's argument is essentially the same as that of Irenaeus, but it is expressed more clearly and logically. The scriptures are the property of the church.

There are three principal arguments which Tertullian employs in proving the sole right of the church to interpret scripture. The first he calls the *praescriptio veritatis*, the prescription of truth. There is a unity of doctrine between the apostles and the apostolic churches which proves that the apostolic churches possess the truth; their teaching is unanimous, and agrees with that of the apostles; the heretics disagree among themselves (*Pr.* 20–30). In the second place, there is the *praescriptio principalitatis*: truth is prior to variations from it, just as the wheat was sown before the devil brought in the tares. In the church the pure wheat is preserved (*Pr.* 31–35). And finally, we have the *praescriptio proprietatis*. The scriptures belonged to us long before heretics thought of using them: "By what right, Marcion, are you cutting trees in my forest? How can you, Valentinus, undertake to change the course of my springs? Who authorizes you, Apelles, to displace my landmarks?" By inheritance from the apostles I possess the scriptures, and I alone (*Pr.* 35–40).

The differentiation among the three types of prescription is more apparent than real. It makes the argument look more impressive; but actually the argument of Tertullian is based on one fact, the actuality of possession. The form in which it is set is based on Roman law, according to which a defendant could request of a magistrate a "prescription," to be placed at the beginning of a bill. This prescription would require the discussion of a preliminary question before the case itself was tried. As Quintilian, writing late in the first century, says, "When the case depends on a prescription, it is not necessary to examine the charge itself."[4] The prescription itself will not win the case; it will merely postpone it, but it may make the plaintiff's position so precarious that he will not consider it worthwhile to continue. Here Tertullian, defending the church's teaching against opponents who claim that it differs from that of scripture, decides to discuss first the question of whose property the scriptures are. Since he believes that in the course of the preliminary examination he can prove them the church's property and at the same time discredit his adversaries, he asks for a prescription.

We have already observed that Irenaeus's insistence on the authority of the church in matters of interpretation does not force him to choose between literal and allegorical exegesis. Depending on the circumstances, he can make use of either method. And so it is with Tertullian. When he believes that the church's faith requires him to find the resurrection of the flesh in scripture, he can insist on a very literal interpretation of the resurrection narrative of Luke while at the same time he explains away Paul's argument in 1 Corinthians as allegory. As d'Alès expresses it:

The dominating tendency in the exegesis of Tertullian is a realism, sometimes extreme, which makes him take everything in a material sense, if not a materialistic sense, and to use the phrase of Bossuet, to corporealize divine things. At the same time that it is excessively realistic, this exegesis is strangely verbal; that is to say, it is intent upon words without always penetrating their meaning.[5]

At the same time, Tertullian's lost work *De spe fidelium* was an "allegorical interpretation," as he himself says (*Adv. Marc.* 3.24). And when the plain meaning of scripture was opposed to his ideas he did not hesitate to interpret it away by allegorization. To his mind there was, of course, no idea of development or of progressive revelation, such as even in his day we find in Clement of Alexandria.[6] And the only way, ultimately, for him to determine whether to interpret a passage literally or to allegorize it was to see whether or not its plain meaning was in accordance with the teaching of the church.

Tertullian set forth orthodoxy as the norm of the interpretation of scripture in the period before Origen became prominent. And, as we have seen, while Origen makes use of the principle of interpretation according to the rule of faith, the meaning of the rule of faith for him is somewhat different from more commonly accepted views, and for him a truly philosophical understanding of scripture was the goal of interpretation. Tertullian detested philosophy and regarded it as the mother of heresy. The authoritative interpretation of scripture was intended to bypass the questions of philosophical interpreters.

But these questions could not be passed by so easily. Even a theologian like Methodius, strongly influenced by Irenaeus and Tertullian and a convinced anti-Origenist, could not return to the simple authoritarianism of Tertullian. Methodius feels the need of justifying the church's exegesis of scripture at the bar of scripture itself. Exegesis must take place "according to the mind of scripture."[7] This principle does not mean that literalism is the only tenable method. Indeed, literalists prove their unbelief when they interpret the Old Testament; they cannot understand the riches of the good things to come. The unfinished tower of Luke 14:28f. suggests to the exegete that his work must be thorough; he must explore the depths of scripture.[8] If scripture has only a literal meaning why did the apostle (Eph. 5:32) take Genesis 2:23f. to refer to Christ and the church? And yet at the same time Methodius is aware of the dangers of an exaggerated allegorization. We must not look for a spiritual interpretation opposed to the literal meaning. Instead, we should follow the guidance of scripture itself, especially the words of Jesus.

Unfortunately Methodius's theory is not always applicable. He has an entire work *De cibis judaicis* in which he shows the allegorical significance of the clean and unclean animals of the Old Testament. He claims that Paul showed him the way when he wrote, "Does God care for oxen?" But while Paul may have been his leader, Methodius' exegesis certainly rejects the literal meaning of scripture. When he finds an unworthy presentation of God, or an absurdity, he feels that this must be allegorized. And yet he is never able to disprove the correctness of literalism. Methodius cannot overcome the tension between two influences which have shaped his thought. These are allegorization and literalism. On the one hand, while refuting Origen he stands fairly close to him; on the other, he would like to prove from scripture the correctness of traditional, authoritative exegesis; and yet he cannot altogether do so.[9]

A far more profound and complete analysis of the relation of scripture to orthodox theology, and of the nature of the exegetical method, is to be found in the *De doctrina christiana* (On Christian teaching) of Augustine. This work was written largely in the year 397. But before discussing it we must examine the way in which a search for the correct exegetical method had influenced Augustine's career. Only when he discovered the allegorical method of interpreting the Old Testament was he able to become a Christian. The principal reason for his hesitation was the fact that the Manichees, among whom he had briefly sojourned, were using literalism in order to discredit the patriarchs of the Old Testament, insisting on the immoralities which scripture imputed to them.

The Manichees asked

> what the source of evil is, and whether God is bounded by a corporeal form and has hair and nails, and whether those men ought to be considered righteous who had many wives at the same time and killed men and made animal sacrifices.[10]

After thus criticizing the Old Testament, they had to defend themselves against the traditional Catholic reply that the God of the Old Testament was the same as the God of the New. They claimed, as Marcion had claimed before them, that the scriptures of the New Testament had been interpolated by advocates of the Jewish Law; and yet, Augustine observed, they had no copies of the pure New Testament available.[11] Marcion had shown more foresight! Augustine already questioned the motives of his Manichaean friends, and he was psychologically prepared to receive the exegetical answer to his problems.

This answer was given by Ambrose, bishop of Milan, in his sermons.[12] Often, in his expositions of the Old Testament, Ambrose would quote Paul's statement, "The letter kills, but the spirit makes alive" (2 Cor. 3:6), and as he explained the difficulties of the Bible, the "mystical veil" was removed from Augustine's eyes. The things which taken literally seemed to teach perversity now could be understood spiritually.[13] And yet the mind of Augustine could not rest in a simple allegorism. Like other interpreters in the orthodox tradition he continued his search for an all-inclusive principle by means of which he could determine what was allegorical and what was not. Moreover, in the course of his theological development he came to take more and more passages of scripture literally. The allegorical method was only a steppingstone towards a final interpretation of scripture.

We are not here concerned with the *De doctrina christiana* in itself, but as an illustration of the authoritative interpretation of scripture. Augustine is no simple traditionalist, yet he upholds the authority of the rule of faith. And, following the teaching of Jesus on the primacy of the law of love (Matt. 22:40), he believes that all scripture must be interpreted in its light:

> If it seems to anyone that he has understood the divine scriptures or any part of them, in such a way that by that understanding he does not build up that double love of God and neighbor, he has not yet understood.[14]

Moreover, the interpreter must explain the mind of the writers of scripture rather than set forth his own opinions. Scripture does not lie. For the understanding of scripture, then, there is need of a wide and deep philological training. This training will prove especially helpful in dealing with ambiguous statements in scripture. The exegete must distinguish between literal and figurative statements. If he is still troubled, he should "consult the rule of faith."[15] If there are two orthodox solutions, he should adopt the one which best suits the context.

While Augustine insists on the need for learning, and attacks the view of those who would like to interpret scripture "without a human guide,"[16] his ultimate authority in interpretation is twofold. It is first of all scripture itself, which at its highest proclaims the law of love as that on which all the rest depends. And in the second place it is the tradition of the church. Augustine takes the insights of Irenaeus and Tertullian and transposes them into a higher key. He is no irrationalist. And yet at the same time he is deeply devoted to the authority of the church.

In the year 434 a priest of the monastery on the island of Lerinum composed a *Commonitorium* in which the authoritative interpretation of scripture received its final exposition in the ancient church. Vincent's general principle has become famous. In the face of heretical aberrations, and the fact that the depth of scripture permits many varying interpretations to be given it,

> the line of the interpretation of the prophets and apostles must be directed according to the norm of the ecclesiastical and Catholic sense.[17]

And what is Catholic? *Quod ubique, quod semper, quod ab omnibus creditum est:* what has been believed everywhere, always, by everyone. There may be a few exceptions—after all, at times the Donatists and the Arians have been in the majority—but this is the general rule.[18] For there is only one gospel, there is only one truth, and it has been handed down in the tradition of the church. There are heretics who hold other views, but their coming was predicted by Moses, who tells of a false prophet who will urge Israel to follow alien gods (Deut. 13:2); in the allegorical language of the Old Testament "alien gods" means "extraneous errors."[19]

This false prophet, Moses said, would arise "in your midst"; therefore we should not be surprised to find even within the church those who have erred from the true interpretation of scripture. Such men have been Origen, who relied too much on his own intellect, and Tertullian, who was insufficiently tenacious of the universal faith.[20] What rule are Catholics to follow in their desire to avoid the temptations which befell such men? They are to remember the words of Paul: "O Timothy, guard the deposit, avoiding the profane novelties of words" (1 Tim. 6:20f.). As Vincent observes, "If novelty is to be avoided, antiquity is to be held; and if novelty is profane, antiquity is sacred."[21]

It might be asked whether any progress is possible in the church of Christ. Certainly there is progress in that faith, but not change. Religion is like the human body, which develops and grows, but remains the same. "It is right for the original dogmas of the heavenly philosophy in the course of time to be cared for, shined, and polished; but it is wrong for them to be changed, truncated, or mutilated."[22]

But the heretics also make great use of scripture. They are always skimming through the Bible. They know that without their array of passages from scripture, they would convince hardly anyone. The apostle Paul predicted their work when he referred to "false apostles, transforming themselves into apostles of Christ" (2 Cor. 11:13). For the true apostles used the Law, the Psalms, and the prophets; so do they. And again Paul says that Satan "transforms himself into an angel of light" (2 Cor. 11:14). This means that the devil himself can quote scripture, a fact which is evident from the story of Jesus' temptation.[23]

In the face of these difficulties what is the Catholic exegete to do? He is to follow the rule set forth at the beginning of Vincent's work; and handed down to him by holy and learned men: they are to interpret the divine canon "according to the traditions of the universal church and according to the rules of Catholic dogma." In effect this interpretation is to be found in the general decrees of a universal council, and also in the consentient opinions of many great masters. This rule is not intended to apply in "every little question of the divine Law" but only in matters concerning the rule of faith. Nor is every heresy to be attacked in this way. Those, however, which are of recent origin and attempt to make use of scripture are to be rejected by this means. Even an Augustine—to whom Vincent guardedly refers—must submit to the authority of the universal church and its tradition.[24]

In the work of Vincent we can recognize the summing up of the authoritative interpretation of scripture. Though he has to condemn Tertullian, he knows the value of his theory of prescription and praises his writings as leading to certain victory over the enemies of the church.[25] And Vincent's theory of tradition is not markedly different from that of his predecessors, including Augustine.[26] He sets forth a theory of legitimate development which permits an advance in the study of the Bible. But his face is set towards the past.

While Vincent refers to the decision of councils and to the consentient interpretations of the fathers, he mentions the authority of the Pope only as a guardian of the deposit. He praises Stephanus, who wrote to the church of Africa: *Nihil novandum, nisi quod traditum est*: No innovation, except from tradition.[27] But papal authority is not for Vincent the ultimate authority. Papal authority in matters of interpretation is first set forth by Alain de Lille, in the late Middle Ages; it is exercised practically rather than theoretically.[28] The Council of Trent does not mention papal authority in proposing the authority of the church as the criterion of interpretation; it merely mentions the sense held by the church and expressed in the unanimous consent of the fathers. But when the Vatican Council of 1870 reiterated the decision of Trent it undoubtedly implied that the authority of the Pope was ultimate.[29]

It is evident that there is a certain tension between the Catholic emphasis on the traditional interpretation of scripture and the efforts of individual exegetes or schools to discover new ways of looking at the Bible. At first glance the slogan *Nihil novandum, nisi quod traditum est* looks reactionary. But if one recognizes the fact that scripture and tradition alike are responses of the church to the Word of God incarnate, as well as the fact of the variety present within the various responses, it is hard to see how the continuity of Christianity can be maintained without something like the slogan or that to which it points. The sentence does not end with the words *nihil novandum*. The possibility of fresh and creative insights remains open. Unless, however, the continuity is maintained it is difficult to understand how the word "Christian" can be employed in describing the insights.

The real question about authority is whether or not it is exercised flexibly. Authority always exists, whether it is that of the church or the churches or a consensus of scholars. The way in which the authority is exercised depends, in large measure, upon the circumstances. In the Roman church itself authoritative pronouncements on biblical questions today are rather different from those made in the heat of the modernist controversy (see chapter 13).

9

The Bible
in the Middle Ages

The theme of biblical interpretation in the Middle Ages is so extensive that it may seem presumptuous to attempt to treat it in one brief chapter. And yet there is little in medieval interpretation that is strikingly novel. As far as interpretation is concerned, the Middle Ages are a period of transition from the old patristic exegetical theology to the divorce between biblical interpretation and theology which we find in the work of Thomas Aquinas. It is this divorce which the Oxford reformers and Martin Luther endeavor to declare invalid.

The materials of biblical study remained largely the same. The form in which the exegetical materials of the past were presented continued to be the *catena*, a chain of interpretations pieced together from the commentaries of the fathers. Usually one principal authority, such as Chrysostom, was followed, and shorter extracts from other interpreters were added. But the variety of the early catenas was largely lost in medieval collections, which were intended to follow "the norm of the ecclesiastical and catholic sense."[1] Moreover the sources of the medieval catenas consisted largely of Latin fathers—Ambrose, Hilary, Augustine, Jerome; the subtlety of Greek exegesis was somewhat disregarded. The *Catena Aurea* of Aquinas, however, makes use of a good many Greek writers.

In the schools of the Carolingian revival another form was developed from the catena. This was the *gloss*. The catena had generally been marginal, sometimes even surrounding the text entirely; the gloss, on the other hand, was sometimes marginal, sometimes interlinear, and sometimes separate and continuous. Later, theological questions were introduced, and finally these questions came to circulate separately. In the late twelfth and early thirteenth centuries in Paris the glosses were taken down by the student and approved by the teacher, whose lectures were based both on the text and on the gloss.[2]

With the use of the gloss in Christian schools we come to another feature of medieval exegesis which might seem to differentiate it from the work of earlier times. This is the fact that scripture study took place in schools, first in those of the Carolingian revival of learning, then in the library of the Victorines in Paris, and finally in the universities. But essentially the study of scripture in schools was not new. We need only remember the work of Origen at Alexandria to realize that this kind of study was being revived rather than invented. The introductory handbooks which were used were thoroughly traditional. Cassiodorus recommends Tyconius, Augustine's *De doctrina christiana*, Adrian, Eucherius, and Junilius;[3] his own work is used by Isidore of Seville, whose work in turn is used by Hugh of St. Victor in his *Didascalicon*—which is fundamentally a reworking of the *De doctrina christiana*![4] Not only were the new handbooks reworkings of old sources; the sources themselves continued to circulate.[5]

Moreover the consultation of Jewish authorities in order to determine the historical sense of a passage was not new. From the time of Theophilus of Antioch there had been a strong Jewish influence on Christian interpreters of the Old Testament; this influence is especially notable in the case of Jerome.[6] But in the twelfth century there was some emphasis in Jewish and Christian exegesis on the historical sense of the Old Testament. This emphasis, as Beryl Smalley has shown, permeates the work of Andrew of St. Victor.[7] He constantly stresses the importance of the historical sense of scripture as his Jewish contemporaries have understood it. For example, in discussing the source of the Hexaemeron in Genesis he says:

> We may believe without absurdity that the holy fathers of old, Adam and his descendants, would commit the Creation carefully to memory, by frequent recital, or even in writing. . . . So it might come to the knowledge of Moses, who sought it by careful research.[8]

At times Andrew's interest in Jewish interpretations led him to disregard the exposition of his Christian predecessors. In discussing Isaiah 7:14–16, which Christians had taken as a prediction of the virginal conception of Jesus, Andrew argues with the Jews, who found a "young woman" rather than a "virgin" in the Hebrew word *'almah*, but does so rather halfheartedly:

> Were we to enter the lists with strength unequal to the doubtful contest, we might perhaps yield. . . . Let us continue the explanation of the literal sense which we had begun.

He then proceeds to give the Jewish interpretation.[9] His contemporary, Richard of St. Victor, wrote a book *De Emmanuele* against this view; and when a disciple of Andrew defended his master, Richard wrote again on the same subject. Andrew is one of two writers in the history of Roman Catholicism who have thus interpreted the passage in Isaiah; the other, in the eighteenth century, retracted his error.[10] In spite of such difficulties, medieval interest in Jewish interpretation did not greatly diminish, although it was not later carried to such lengths.

The most important and characteristic method of biblical interpretation, however, was not literal but allegorical. In the late patristic period and in the Middle Ages, a system of allegorization was developed according to which four meanings were to be sought in every text. Sometimes there were as many as seven, but the more normal number of senses was four.[11] A little verse in circulation as late as the sixteenth century illustrates these senses.

Littera gesta docet, quid credas allegoria,
Moralis quid agas, quo tendas anagogia.
(The letter shows us what God and our fathers did;
The allegory shows us where our faith is hid;
The moral meaning gives us rules of daily life;
The anagogy shows us where we end our strife.)

Though this classification was widespread in the Middle Ages, it comes originally from the time of Augustine and John Cassian. Its use can best be shown in the example of Galatians 4:22ff. Here "Jerusalem" can be understood in four different ways. Historically it means the city of the Jews; allegorically it signifies the church of Christ; anagogically it points to that heavenly city which is the mother of us all; and tropologically (or morally) it indicates the human soul. This fourfold understanding of "Jerusalem" became standard and it is found not only throughout the Middle Ages, but also as late as Nicholas of Lyra and in the early works of Luther and Melanchthon.[12]

In actual practice many interpreters limited their investigations to two senses, while some of the most famous medieval exegetes interpreted scripture in terms of three. But in the ninth century Rabanus Maurus developed a theory of the importance of the number four, and at a later date Franciscan number-mysticism encouraged the use of the fourfold interpretation. Many Franciscans considered all four senses of scripture to be of equal importance. Such Dominicans as Albertus Magnus and Thomas Aquinas, however, insisted that the literal meaning should be the basis of the other three. It is impossible to distinguish interpretations according to the orders of friars; the Franciscan Bonaventure insisted on the primacy of the literal sense, while the Dominican Hugo of St. Cher, like Dante, regarded all four as equal.

The reason for this insistence on the multiplicity of senses in scripture was twofold. In the first place, in the early Middle Ages and for many writers even later, no adequate theory of the relation of revelation to reason had been worked out. Throughout the patristic period theology had been largely a matter of exegesis. Theological systems were attempts to interpret as broadly as possible the words of God in scripture. But natural theology was used as sparingly as possible. It was therefore necessary to discover predicted and prefigured in scripture whatever insights God had vouchsafed to his people. According to Cassiodorus the Psalms were full of the liberal arts. In the second place, not only through the Greek fathers but also through Augustine the "vitality of Platonism" had been able to influence the Christian world view, and it was usually believed that, as Smalley expresses it, "Scripture, like the visible world, is a great mirror reflecting God, and therefore all and every kind of truth."[13] God's words and God's will were not expressed in scripture, but hidden in it. Scripture was like the medieval cathedral, which spoke to the people in a language of symbols.

There were other interpreters who were not content to read the symbols and understand the nature of God and man, but instead tried to penetrate the mysteries of history. Following Rupert of

Deutz, who had set forth the traditional Christian interpretation of history in his interpretations of scripture, a Cistercian monk named Joachim of Flora found the Old Testament a book of the Father, the New Testament a book of the Son, and the future age, not yet arrived, the age of the Holy Spirit. As John the Baptist had prepared for the coming of the Son, so Joachim believed, Benedict had prepared for the coming of the Spirit. This interpretation of scripture might have been only a harmless example of monastic enthusiasm had not a young Franciscan in 1254 written an introduction to it, arguing that Joachim's works were the gospel of the Holy Spirit. The spiritual Franciscans adopted the dead Joachim as their own; they held that he had been the new Elijah, doing the work of the Baptist for the Spirit. The new age, they calculated, would begin in 1270. Unfortunately, about that time their understanding of scripture was condemned by a papal commission.[14] A new and more reliable method of exegesis was on its way.

There had already been a considerable decline in the importance of the allegorical interpretation. We have seen that Andrew of St. Victor ignored it almost entirely; and an interesting example of the reaction from allegorism is found in the remark of a critic who had been told that the red color of the sacrificial cow pretypified the blood of the passion of Christ. "It would be all the same," he said, "if the cow had been black; the allegory is worthless; whatever the color of the cow, some sort of allegory could be found for it."[15] The allegorical interpretation survived largely in preaching. But for a rational, almost rationalistic, theological method such a subjective attitude towards scripture could not prove satisfactory. What did God mean to say in his word? Did he intend to conceal his meaning, or did he intend to express it? The Aristotelian view of nature, which the newer theologians were adopting, did not encourage the idea of symbolism. And for this reason, among others, the literal meaning of scripture came to be regarded more highly.

The principal exponent of the importance of the literal sense of scripture is St. Thomas Aquinas, the most influential philosophical theologian of the Catholic church. The meaning of scripture is of especial importance to him because, while he makes use of philosophical understanding as much as is possible he recognizes the primacy of revelation as contained in scripture:

Sacred doctrine makes use also of the authority of philosophers in those questions in which they were able to know the truth by natural reason, as Paul quotes a saying of Aratus [Acts 17:28]. Nevertheless, sacred doctrine makes use of these authorities as extrinsic and probable arguments, but properly uses the authority of the canonical scriptures as an incontrovertible proof. . . . For our faith rests upon the revelation made to the apostles and prophets, who wrote the canonical books, and not on the revelations (if there be any) made to other doctors.[16]

Scripture alone is free from error; and therefore we must be sure of what it says. It uses metaphors, to be sure; but those metaphors can easily and naturally be understood:

It is natural to man to attain to intellectual truths through sensible objects, because all our knowledge originates through sense. Hence in holy scripture spiritual truths are fittingly taught under the likeness of material things.[17]

The difference between this explanation and the outlook of Clement or Origen is very marked. They would have agreed with Aquinas in their search for "spiritual truths." Both he and they have an intellectualist approach to scripture. Yet in his understanding of the way in which this approach is to be undertaken he stands far closer to the school of Antioch than to the Alexandrines. This difference should not be exaggerated, however; Aquinas does not reject the allegorical interpretation, and in a way both Alexandria and Antioch can claim him as their heir.

His explanation of the importance of the literal sense of scripture is set forth most fully in the *Summa theologica*.[18] It will perhaps be somewhat more clear for the modern reader if Thomas' own view is quoted first. It takes as its text the statement of Gregory in his *Moralia* (20:1): "Holy scripture by the manner of its speech transcends every science, because in one and the same sentence, while it describes a fact, it reveals a mystery."

The author of holy scripture is God, in whose power it is to signify his meaning, not by words only (as man also can do) but by things themselves. So, whereas in every other science things are signified by words, this science has the property that the things signified by the words have themselves also a signification. Therefore that first signification whereby words signify things belongs to the first sense, the historical or literal. That signification whereby things signified by words have themselves also a signification is called the spiritual sense, which is based on the literal, and presupposes it. For as the apostle says (Heb. 10:1) the Old Law is a figure of the New Law and (Pseudo-) Dionysius says: "The New Law itself is a figure of future glory." Again, in the New Law, whatever our Head has done is a type of what we ought to do. Therefore, so far as the things of the Old Law signify the things of the New Law, there is the allegorical sense; so far as the things done in Christ, or so far as the things which signify Christ, are types of what we ought to do, there is the moral sense. But so far as they signify what relates to eternal glory, there is the anagogical sense. Since the literal sense is that which the author intends, and since the author of holy scripture is God, it is not unfitting, as Augustine says, if even according to the literal sense one word in holy scripture should have several senses.

What Aquinas means in his last sentence is apparently not that there are several literal senses of scripture but that the literal sense is the basis for the other senses, which can properly be built upon it.

Three objections are raised to the teaching that it is possible to have several senses in scripture. The first is the most serious. "Many different senses in one text produce confusion and deception and destroy all force of argument. Hence no argument, but only fallacies, can be deduced from a multiplicity of propositions. But holy scripture ought to be able to state the truth without any fallacy. Therefore . . ." Aquinas's reply insists on the primacy of the literal sense.

> The multiplicity of these senses does not produce equivocation or any other kind of multiplicity, seeing that these senses are not multiplied because one word signifies several things; but because the things signified by the words can themselves be types of other things. Thus in holy scripture no confusion results, for all the senses are founded on one—the literal—from which alone can any argument be drawn, and not from those intended in allegory, as Augustine says. Nevertheless, nothing of holy scripture perishes on account of this, since nothing necessary to faith is contained under the spiritual sense which is not elsewhere put forward by the scripture in its literal sense.

This marks theology's declaration of independence from the allegorical method.

The second objection merely points to the confusion and lack of system in the allegorical method and asks how it can be used. Augustine's four senses do not seem to be the same as the four commonly employed. Aquinas contents himself with explaining what Augustine meant and contrasting it with the classification of Hugh of St. Victor. The third objection is a complaint against the fourfold division; the parabolical sense has been overlooked. Aquinas replies that the parabolical sense is contained in the literal. The literal sense is concerned with the meaning of words, which can be used both properly and figuratively. The literal sense is not the figure, but the thing which is meant. Thus the literal meaning of "the arm of God" is not that God has an arm, but the meaning of the expression "operative power." Aquinas concludes that "nothing false can even underlie the literal sense of holy scripture." Anthropomorphism cannot claim that it understands the scriptures at all.

An example of his literal interpretation may be found in his treatment of the traditional question of the nature of the garden of Eden. From the earliest days of the church interpreters had been divided; some held that there was a real garden on earth, others that it was spiritual. Thomas says that "the things which are said of Paradise in scripture are set forth by means of an historical narrative. Now in everything which scripture thus sets forth the truth (of the story) must be taken as a foundation and upon it spiritual expositions are to be built." Indeed Aquinas's exposition of the eighth chapter of Isaiah was so literal that a later commentator calls it a "Jewish exposition, quite unworthy of St. Thomas' mind."[19]

The results of this late medieval insistence on the literal interpretation of scripture were incalculable. In the first place, an immediate impetus was given to the study of Hebrew and the production of literal and historical commentaries on the Old Testament. More important was the rejection of the patristic theological method with the divorce of theology from exegesis. The divorce was followed immediately, if not preceded, by the remarriage of theology to philosophy. Nevertheless, there remained children of the first marriage who were not satisfied with their new father. Several facts point towards this conclusion. Scholasticism triumphed only gradually; even after the need for allegorization seemed past, Nicholas of Lyra set forth the spiritual as well as the literal sense in his commentaries; and the Reformation claimed to be a return to the method of theology through exegesis.

Along with the emphasis on historical studies came the claim of objectivity. No longer could the interpreter claim to be directly inspired by God in the setting forth of his exegesis. All knowledge comes through the senses, and the interpretation of scripture requires no special inner grace. Here again we see that medieval philosophy is more rationalistic than either the fathers or the Reformation; it stands close, as a matter of fact, to such a philosopher as Spinoza. And we shall observe that Luther turns to the traditional inner understanding of scripture, as does Colet of St. Paul's.

In the medieval claim of objectivity we find the beginning of modern scientific study of the scriptures. Reason is set up as an autonomous agent. The countless subtle meanings which the ingenuity of Christian Platonists found in scripture were all brushed aside in the rejection of the theory of hidden symbols. The followers of Aquinas found it touching that when he died he had been dictating an exposition of the Song of Songs and had just reached the verse, "Daughters of Jerusalem, say to my beloved that I die of love." But it was merely touching. There was no longer any profound significance in the fact. Thomas's love of symbolism is reflected only in his Eucharistic hymns.

10

The Bible
and the Reformation

It is almost a truism to say that modern historical study of the Bible could not have come into existence without the Reformation. We must not overstate the case. In the sixteenth century there were two great movements of the human spirit, not one; and historical exegesis is even more the child of the Renaissance than of the Reformation. But Protestant interpretation of the Bible, whether historical or not, owes its life to the spirit of the Reformation. Catholic exegesis relies strongly on the authority of the fathers. It interprets the Bible by the tradition of the church. Protestant exegesis makes a fresh start, often overturning the accumulated decisions of centuries. For to the Protestant spirit the Bible is not a book of law like the American Constitution, interpreted by judicial decisions which possess binding force. It is a book of life through which God speaks directly to the human soul. The spirit of the Reformation is diametrically opposed to the authoritative interpretation of the Bible.

While the reformers, from John Wyclif on, emphasized the literal and grammatical interpretation of scripture, they were not innovating. As we have seen, Aquinas held a view very much like theirs. But they differ from him and from the overwhelming majority of ancient exegetes in their insistence on the right of the text, as literally interpreted, to stand alone. Scripture for the reformers is not one of several pillars which uphold the house of faith; it is the sole foundation. And the reformers were willing to insist on their understanding of the Bible no matter what previous exegetes might have said, no matter whether they contradicted even the decisions of councils. The church was not to be the arbiter of the meaning of scripture, for scripture, the word of God, was the church's judge. Naturally the reformers insisted on an historical, literal, grammatical understanding of the Bible as they came to believe that a new authority must be set up to oppose the authority of the church.

But their exegesis was never merely historical. It began in the letter but it necessarily proceeded under the guidance of the Spirit. And by the light of the Spirit, they believed, the religious value of scripture could be at once defined and transmitted. Luther insists on the primacy of those books which "preach Christ," for Christ, the very Word of God, is himself the content of the word of God in the Bible. Such a view requires the typological understanding of the Old Testament, and often permits allegorical interpretation to establish proofs of the authority of the church; Christ is above any merely human authority. And

> no believing Christian can be forced to recognize any authority beyond the sacred scripture, which is exclusively invested with divine right, unless, indeed, there comes a new and attested revelation.[1]

Such a view, representing an almost complete break with the conceptions of authority prevalent in earlier theological systems, deserves careful analysis. How did it arise? What were the pressures which brought it into existence? What theory of interpretation was the final result? We must examine the Reformation interpretation of scripture as we find it especially in the work of Martin Luther.

It must be admitted that Luther had many forerunners, men who were eager to put the Bible into the hands of the people and translate it into the vernacular.[2] John Wyclif was such a man. Luther also had contemporaries and successors among the radical reformers who were determined in various ways not so much to reform the church as to create it anew on the basis of what they understood it to have been in New Testament times. Millenarian and perfectionist interpretations, recalling to some extent the Gnostic views of earlier ages, flourished in the sixteenth century. But Luther's work, at least for the right-wing majority among Protestants, was more significant than theirs. His battle, which at first dealt only with such questions as the merits of scholastic theology and of the sale of indulgences, gradually came to be concerned with the principles of interpretation. For a thousand years, it seemed, the church had safeguarded its theological systems and institutions by authoritative exegesis and allegorization, often fanciful, of uncomfortable words in scripture. Now the reformer struck where ecclesiastical armor was weak. He knew its weakness from personal experience:

> When I was a monk, I was an expert in allegories. I allegorized everything. Afterwards through the Epistle to the Romans I came to some knowledge of Christ. There I saw that allegories were not what Christ meant but what Christ was.[3]

After 1517, when Luther definitely broke with the Roman church, he ceased to make use of allegorization, and insisted on the necessity of "one simple solid sense" for the arming of theologians against Satan. He admits the existence of allegories in scripture, but they are to be found only where the various authors intended them. Therefore a historical understanding of the author and of his times is essential to the exegete. This historical understanding, as he points out in the preface to his commentary on Isaiah, gives us the primary meaning of the text. It is clearly associated with knowledge of the scriptures as a whole, by means of which the ordinary expressions and idioms of scripture can be grasped.

But the historical and grammatical interpretation is not an end in itself. It is a means to the understanding of Christ, who is taught in all the books of the Bible. "Christ is the point in the circle from which the whole circle is drawn."[4] Here Luther returns to a considerable degree to the Christocentric interpretation found in the New Testament itself. And he introduces an element into his exegesis which takes it beyond "objective" philosophical interpretation into the subjective realm of faith. For how otherwise is one to determine which passages effectively "preach Christ" and which do not, except by faith? His own emphasis on the Pauline epistles, especially Romans and Galatians, as containing the truest gospel, reveals the subjective emphasis of his thought.

This subjective element is found not only in his acceptance or rejection of books from the central place in the Bible, but also in his general exegetical theory:

> Experience is necessary for the understanding of the Word. It is not merely to be repeated or known, but to be lived and felt.[5]

Our experience under the guidance of faith leads us beyond philology to a "spiritual interpretation" of the Bible. The second is not opposed to the first, but is built upon it. As Luther wrote, two days before his death:

> No one can understand Virgil in the Bucolics and Georgics, unless for five years he has been a shepherd or a farmer. No one understands Cicero in the epistles (so I presume), unless for twenty years he has held some important office of state. No one should think that he has sufficiently tasted the holy scriptures, unless for a hundred years he has governed churches with the prophets.[6]

But Luther does not mean simply that experience in religion brings comprehension of the scriptures. It is an essential; but the Holy Spirit brings its illumination to the mind of the exegete who is searching for the Christocentric meaning. "God must say to you in your heart, This is God's word."[7] We are to understand the words of scripture "in their kernel and feel them in the heart."[8]

How subjective is this understanding? Luther certainly believed that the scriptures, at least in their fundamental Christological messages, were sufficiently clear for everyone to understand. And he apparently thought that there could be unanimity in the theory that Romans and Galatians, the Fourth Gospel and 1 Peter contain the kernel of Christianity. His translation of the Bible by its freedom in paraphrasing shows how little doubt he had as to the perspicuity of its essential meaning. "There is not on earth," he says, "a book more lucidly written than the Holy Scripture."[9] The Bible can be understood in terms of itself—*scriptura scripturae interpres*—and no patristic commentary is necessary:

> This is the true touchstone by which all books are to be judged, when one sees whether they urge Christ or not, as all scripture shows forth Christ, and St. Paul will know no one but Christ [1 Cor. 2:2].[10]

Is this subjective "spiritual" interpretation, the glory of the Reformation, religiously valid? If it is, any Christian may read scripture under the Spirit's guidance. Because the spiritual interpretation is based on literal and historical exegesis, he or she can make use of the fathers insofar as they were competent exegetes. Of legal authority they retain none.

Not all the reformers carried the principles of Reformation exegesis to the conclusion which Luther reached. John Calvin, for example, vigorously maintains an "objective" type of interpretation. For him, scripture itself is the authority for Christian belief, rather than any Christocentric interpretation of scripture. In the *Institutes of the Christian Religion* Calvin sets forth his theory of exegesis. With Aquinas he rejects the use of allegorization in dogmatic theology.[11] The Bible

> obtains the same complete credit and authority with believers, when they are satisfied of its divine origin, as if they heard the very words pronounced by God Himself.[12]

The authority of scripture is prior to that of the church, for the apostle says that the church is built on the foundation of the apostles and prophets. Their doctrine is therefore older than the church itself. (The accuracy of this statement, based on Ephesians 2:20, can be questioned both exegetically and historically. Exegetically, the apostle is addressing gentile converts to Christianity, who were "built upon" the apostles and prophets. Historically, the doctrine of apostles and prophets is not "older" than the church; it *is* the doctrine of the church.)

How are we to prove that scripture is the Word of God? "The principal proof of the scriptures is everywhere derived from the character of the Divine Speaker." Rational argument is not only audacious but also unconvincing. Ultimately faith must determine our acceptance of the Bible. And faith is not a possession of everyone. "Whenever we are disturbed at the paucity of believers, let us . . . remember that none but those to whom it was given have any apprehension of the mysteries of God." The truth of their exegesis is confirmed by the "internal testimony of the Holy Spirit."

By his acceptance of the primacy of faith in exegesis Calvin opened the way for subjectivism even while he tried to exclude it. In actual practice, however, he refused to read his theological views into his interpretation of scripture, and even criticized the evangelists for their apparent "twisting" of the Old Testament.[13] It might well be claimed that in thus distinguishing exegesis from theology he was untrue to the fundamental Reformation principle of theology by exegesis. Luther forcefully expresses this principle:

> This is the golden age of theology. It cannot rise higher, because we

have come so far as to sit in judgment on all the doctors of the
church and test them by the judgment of the apostles and prophets.[14]

The later Reformation did not follow Luther, however, and it came
to insist on the traditional principle of verbal inspiration and infallibility which had been alien to him.[15] Scripture no longer speaks
to the heart but to the critical intellect. It is used for the reconstruction of dogmatic systems. Protestant orthodoxy in the seventeenth
century becomes as rigid as any medieval theological construction.

At the Reformation the church of England also accepted the new
principle of the primacy of scripture. The sixth of the Thirty-nine
Articles of Religion states that, "Holy Scripture containeth all
things necessary to salvation," and the eighth shows the primacy
of the Bible even to the creeds by urging their acceptance on the
ground that "they may be proved by most certain warrants of Holy
Scripture." Both deacons and priests are required at ordination to
proclaim their belief in the sufficiency of holy scriptures; and in
the nineteenth article it is pointed out that the churches of Jerusalem, Alexandria, Antioch, and Rome have erred "in matters of
Faith." The Bible is the supreme authority for the doctrine of the
English church. The first of the homilies set forth in the Elizabe-
than period stresses the necessity of reading "God's Words" under
the guidance of "some godly doctor" and the Holy Spirit. "God
Himself from above will give light unto our minds." Another homily[16] explains that difficulties in scripture are not without meaning. "Let us . . . endeavor ourselves to search out the wisdom hidden in the outward bark of the Scriptures."

At the same time, the appeal to tradition was not abandoned.
The Preface to the Ordinal (1550) claims that the threefold ministry of bishops, priests, and deacons is validated not by scripture
alone but also by "ancient authors," or, in other words, the early
fathers. And this combination of scripture with ancient authors is
to be understood by all those who are "diligently reading" and
therefore recognize that the ministry is both apostolic and contemporary. The supremacy of scripture was generally recognized;[17]
but appeals to the fathers occur even within the Articles.

The Reformation principle of scripture also had some influence
among Roman Catholics. Blaise Pascal does not stand directly un-

der the influence of the Reformation, and yet he is not a traditionalist Catholic. His religious thought is formed by his study of the
Bible, and we may mention him here as one who profited by the
work of the reformers. He almost echoes Luther in his famous declaration concerning the nature of God:

> God of Abraham, God of Isaac, God of Jacob, not of the philoso-
> phers and scholars.[18]

Pascal's God is the God revealed in scripture; and he interprets
scripture with the heart:

> It is the heart which feels God and not the reason. That is what faith
> is—God sensible to the heart, not to the reason.[19]

Such an interpretation of scripture, like that of Luther, is essentially neither literal nor allegorical. In the Bible "there is enough
clarity to enlighten the elect and enough obscurity to humble
them."[20] It is a book of paradox. Ordinary authors have one meaning; it has one meaning, too, but one which reconciles all its contradictions. This meaning is found in Jesus Christ.[21]

Pascal is a Catholic who is deeply influenced by the spiritual re-
newal of the Reformation. He cannot go all the way with the reformers; he still clings to the authority of the church, even in the
interpretation of scripture.[22] But he shows the way in which the
new wine of Christocentric interpretation can stretch the old wineskins of patristic exegesis, even for one who still clings to the authoritative interpretations of scripture.

The Reformation interpretation of the Bible, as we have seen,
was given classical expression by Martin Luther. He rejects the
traditional interpretation, for it stands in the way of our personal
understanding of scripture:

> The teachings of the father are useful only to lead us to the scrip-
> tures, as they were led, and then we must hold to the scriptures
> alone.[23]

The resulting exegesis certainly is subjective; but it is also objective. It is based on the literal meaning of the biblical writings:

> No violence is to be done to the words of God, whether by man or
> angel; but they are to be retained in their simplest meaning wherever
> possible, and to be understood in their grammatical and literal sense

unless the context plainly forbids, lest we give our adversaries occasion to make a mockery of all the scriptures. Thus Origen was repudiated, in olden times, because he despised the grammatical sense and turned the trees, and all else written concerning Paradise, into allegories; for it might therefrom be concluded that God did not create trees.[24]

The Bible is not one standard of authority among others, as it was for medieval Catholicism. It is the sole standard. And it is not an objective standard, as it was for Thomas Aquinas. It is a standard at once objective and subjective, for in it and through it God himself speaks to the human heart. The Bible authenticates itself.[25]

In Luther's insistence on the subjective element in interpretation we are close to modern theories of exegesis which stress the ultimate impossibility of "objective" analysis of human thought. At the same time Luther marks a return to more ancient, less rationalistic exegetical methods. He restores exegesis to theology. He endeavors to invalidate the divorce which took place in the Middle Ages. And his contribution has permanent value for the interpretation of scripture. Not only the nineteenth-century critics, but also their opponents, could claim him as their prophet.

11

The Rise
of Rationalism

The fifteenth century was a time of great intellectual ferment; it was a time when small skirmishes and abortive revolts prepared the way for the revolution which was to come. The questioning of traditional authority, to be sure, was no greater than the questioning which had existed in previous periods. But the authority of the Catholic church had diminished as a result of rising rationalism. Indeed, the church had encouraged the development of rational opposition by its insistence on the rationality of faith. Now human reason turned to attack authority and to insist on its own freedom.

Two figures, more or less within the church, illustrate this trend. The first is a man of the Italian Renaissance: Lorenzo Valla, secretary to the king of Naples. In 1440 his work *De falso credita et ementita Constantini donatione* made him so uneasy that he fled to Barcelona to escape the anticipated wrath of Rome. Papal authority for centuries had rested secure on the presumed legal basis of the "donation of Constantine"; now Valla had proved it a forgery. He had overestimated the anger of the papal court, however, and soon was able to return safely to Italy. There he continued his literary investigations. He found that the supposed letter of Christ to Abgar, king of Edessa, which such church historians as Eusebius had believed genuine, was spurious; he criticized the Latin style of the Vulgate; he finally questioned the authenticity of the Apostles' Creed. Even a weakened Rome could not tolerate such conclusions, and Valla was summoned before the Inquisition. Nothing illustrates more plainly the extent to which the traditional authority of the Catholic church had been modified than the fact that his trial was dropped. What did he say to his investigators? He believed as Mother church believed. He could not resist adding that it was quite true that she knew nothing. But he hastily reiterated his profession of belief. The schism between faith and knowledge was well under way. And under Nicholas V, Valla became Apostolic Writer at the papal court. He died peacefully in 1457.

The other rebel against traditional authority was even more highly placed within the church. This was Reginald Pecock, bishop of St. Asaph and Chichester in England. His *Rule of Christian Religion* brought much more trouble upon him than Valla's work occasioned in Italy. He was tried before an ecclesiastical court and threatened with death unless he recanted. And he was willing to do so, for his theories had been occasioned at least in part by controversies with the Lollards, simple believers who insisted on a literal interpretation of scripture and attacked the church. It was also the case that Pecock was happiest when living in Oxford, and that he was prominent in the stirring intellectual life of the university. The claims of reason seemed very strong to him. What he had said was that even ecumenical decrees of the church were subject to error; therefore they had to be proved from the Bible. The interpretation of the Bible itself had to be made in the light of human reason. It has sometimes been thought that Pecock was a forerunner of the Reformation, but nothing was farther from his mind. He was a daring apologist who believed in the complete rationality of the church's faith if properly understood. Other churchmen were not so certain.

In the sixteenth century the influence of ancient literature and modern intellectualism became even more pronounced. It was a new type of intellectualism, however. Scholasticism seemed pallid compared with the fresh insights of philology. The study of the fathers showed that there were vast areas of Christian thought which had not come down in the tradition. Naturally there was resistance. At Oxford there were non-Greeks who called themselves Trojans, and insisted that theology alone was of importance. But the ablest men were to be found on the side of the new learning. Thomas More says:

> How can he know theology if he is ignorant of Hebrew and Greek and Latin? He thinks, I presume, that it can all be found in the scholastic conundrums. Those I admit can be learned with no particular effort. But theology, that august queen of heaven, demands an ampler scope. The knowledge of God can be gathered only out of

scripture, scripture and the early Catholic fathers. That was where
for a thousand years the searchers after truth looked for it and found
it, before these modern paradoxes were heard of.[1]

The movement was one of great enthusiasm. Erasmus wrote to
John Colet, who was to become dean of St. Paul's:

> Theology is the mother of sciences. But nowadays the good and the
> wise keep clear of it, and leave the field to the dull and sordid, who
> think themselves omniscient. You have taken arms against these
> people. You are trying to bring back the Christianity of the apostles,
> and clear away the thorns and briars with which it is overgrown.[2]

Its members disagreed, however, in their attitude towards medieval exegetes and theologians. Erasmus considered Thomas Aquinas incomparable, while Colet said that he "would not have laid
down the law so boldly on all things in heaven and earth if he had
not been an arrogant fool, and he would not have so contaminated
Christianity with his preposterous philosophy if he had not been a
worldling at heart." This same divergence is found in their views
of the interpretation of scripture.

Erasmus was much more a traditionalist than Colet. While on
the one hand he produced a new edition and translation of the New
Testament with notes which turned its denunciations against his
contemporaries, he insisted that there were many senses in scripture. "We might as well read Livy as Judges or other parts of the
Old Testament if we leave out the allegorical meaning." And he
admired the *Catena Aurea* of Aquinas. Colet, on the other hand,
insisted on the literal interpretation of scripture. The Holy Spirit
brings forth in us one understanding of his words.

> In the writings of the New Testament, except when it pleased the
> Lord Jesus and his apostles to speak in parables, as Christ often does
> in the gospels and St. John throughout in the Revelation, all the rest
> of the discourse, in which either the Savior teaches his disciples
> more plainly, or the apostles instruct the churches, has the sense that
> appears on the surface; nor is one thing said and another meant, but
> the very thing is meant which is said, and the sense is wholly literal.
> Still, inasmuch as the Church of God is figurative, conceive always
> an *anagoge* in what you hear in the doctrines of the Church. . . .[3]

This moderation, which Thomas Aquinas would not have found

unattractive, is not retained in the treatment of the Old Testament. There, allegorization is permitted. But Colet's allegorizations are not numerous, and they usually come from traditional typology.

Neither Erasmus nor Colet had any desire other than to be reformers of the church while remaining its servants. Like Aquinas, like Pecock, they believed that the truth which their reason found in ancient manuscripts was not different from the truth which the church's faith had handed down. Colet's education, admiringly set forth by Erasmus, casts considerable light on their attitude. The young Colet was fascinated by Cicero, Plato, Plotinus. When he turned to Christian writers he disliked the scholastics and Augustine, but greatly enjoyed Pseudo-Dionysius, Origen, Cyprian, Ambrose, and Jerome. Insofar as he was a humanist, he was a Christian humanist.

The attitude of these reformers towards the interpretation of scripture is not strikingly different from that of their predecessors. They are eager to insist on the relevance of scripture for their own time, and therefore stress its literal meaning; but they do not deny that it may have other meanings as well. And they do not directly question the authority of the church. Nevertheless, in their work the ground is broken for an interpretation of scripture by exegetes who stand entirely outside, for whom reason is the only guide. The gradual diffusion of an attitude of questioning towards the Bible may be seen in two examples from the late sixteenth century. A ploughwright named Matthew Hamond was tried in 1579 by the bishop and consistory of Norwich on the charge that he had "denied Christ"; and one of the principal items in the accusation was this: he had said "that the New Testament and gospel of Christ are but mere foolishness, a story of men, or rather a mere fable." Hamond was burned. Five years later John Hilton, no simple ploughwright but a clerk in holy orders, was tried for having said in a sermon in St. Martin-in-the-Fields, London, that the Old and New Testaments were fables. He abjured and was able to escape the fate of the less tactful Hamond.[4]

Such a free criticism of the narratives of scripture takes us back to the age of the great opponents of Christianity, Celsus, Porphyry, and the emperor Julian. Indeed, its origins can be traced still further back into the Hellenistic age where we find systematic rationalistic criticism of Greek mythology. The recovery of classical literature and the higher value placed upon it by the Renaissance undoubtedly encouraged a critical attitude towards the Bible.[5] Moreover, the rise of philosophy as an autonomous science and its gradual divorce from theology made possible and indeed made necessary a fresh evaluation of the meaning and interpretation of the Bible. At the same time, Protestant bibliolatry raised questions in thinking men's minds. When they heard the writers of scripture called "amanuenses of God, hands of Christ, scribes and notaries of the Holy Spirit, living and writing pens,"[6] they might wonder whether papal authority had been any more rigorous. As the Anglican Richard Hooker says:

> As incredible praises given to men do often abate and impair the credit of the deserved commendation, so we must likewise take great heed lest by attributing to scripture more than it can have, the incredibility of that do cause even those things which it hath abundantly to be less reverently esteemed.[7]

In the seventeenth century the esteem of scripture was less reverent than had been the case in the past.

Two philosophers will serve as examples of the growing influence of rationalism and the declining authority of scripture and of the church. In 1651 Thomas Hobbes published in Paris his *Leviathan*, a study of "the matter, form and power of a commonwealth, ecclesiastical and civil." In this work he exhibits typical Anglican caution, rejecting continental biblicism and Roman rigor at the same time. Against Protestant exaltation of scripture he writes:

> When God speaketh to man, it must be either immediately, or by mediation of another man. . . . To say that God hath spoken to him in the Holy Scripture is not to say that God hath spoken to him immediately but by mediation of the prophets or of the apostles or of the church, in such manner as he speaks to all other Christian men [ch. 32].

Here Hobbes anticipates the modern theory that the Bible is not itself the revelation of God but the record of that revelation. He further minimizes the authority of scripture by insisting on the importance of the canon. The church has chosen those books which it regards as the rules of Christian life. But against Roman Catholicism Hobbes is equally emphatic. After observing that spiritual darkness results from the misinterpretation of scripture, he points out against the Roman apologist Bellarmine that

> the greatest and main abuse of scripture, and to which almost all the rest are either consequent or subservient, is the wresting of it to prove that the kingdom of God mentioned so often in the scripture is the present Church [ch. 44].

The next chapter, "Of Demonology and Other Relics of the Religion of the Gentiles," is an attack on the Roman church.

Hobbes's interest is not in scripture as a revelation of God's action in history or as a source of Christian theology. He is a political philosopher, and he regards scripture as the book which contains the rules and regulations and moral principles of the ecclesiastical commonwealth. In the late Middle Ages it had been shown that scripture could be divorced from theology. Now it was the turn of philosophy to see what use could be made of the Bible. And the most important systematic development of a philosophical analysis is found in the work of Benedict Spinoza.

Spinoza devotes a large part of his *Tractatus Theologico-Politicus* to the question of the relation of theology to philosophy. His answer was considered so dangerous that he found it advisable to publish it anonymously in Hamburg in 1670; in 1674 the book was prohibited by the States-General, and it was also placed on the Index. There was a practical occasion for his work. Spinoza had been born during the Thirty Years' War; Europe was still in a chaotic state because of the clash of theologies; and Spinoza believed that the "animosity and hatred" of Christians might be ended by a careful separation of the spheres of theology and philosophy. Then reason might guide men's minds to truth and wisdom while theology continued to bring forth piety and obedience. The fundamental error in the interpretation of scripture had been men's desire to find philosophy in it:

> I grant that they [the Christians] are never tired of professing their wonder at the profound mysteries of holy scripture; still I cannot discover that they teach anything but speculations of Platonists and Ar-

istotelians, to which (in order to save their credit for Christianity) they have made holy scripture conform; not content to rave with the Greeks themselves, they want to make the prophets rave also [Preface].

The result is that Christians give formal assent to the scriptures rather than possess a living faith, and they are forced to despise reason. Spinoza, desiring to liberate them from this bondage, determines to examine scripture "afresh in a careful, impartial and unfettered spirit, making no assumptions concerning it." He has the advantage of belonging to the race which wrote the Bible, and he can understand the way in which they write:

I must . . . premise that the Jews never make any mention or account of secondary or particular causes, but in a spirit of religion, piety, and what is commonly called godliness, refer all things directly to the Deity. For instance, if they make money by a transaction, they say God gave it to them; if they desire anything they say that God has disposed their hearts towards it; if they think anything, they say God told them. Hence we must not suppose that everything is prophecy or revelation which is described in scripture as told by God to anyone [ch. 1].

By means of this principle Spinoza is able to undermine the authority of scripture as revelation or even as record of revelation; for obviously at any point where a divine decree or action seemed irrational, it could be claimed that Hebrew idiom was responsible for its attribution to God. The result of his investigation shows the complete rationality of the biblical revelation:

I found nothing taught expressly by scripture which does not agree with our understanding, or which is repugnant thereto, and as I saw that the prophets taught nothing which is not very simple and easily to be grasped by all, and further, that they clothed their teaching in the style, and confirmed it with the reasons, which would most deeply move the mind of the masses to devotion toward God, I became thoroughly convinced that the Bible leaves reason absolutely free, that it has nothing in common with philosophy, in fact, that revelation and philosophy stand on totally different footings [ch. 1].

The result of this conviction is the absolute freedom of human reason, released from the claims of theology. Theology is moral theology. "Revelation has obedience for its sole object." Naturally, the question of miracle can be answered with considerable ease, by means of the general principle that scripture, written by Jews, does not discuss secondary causes. It

> only narrates events in the order and the style which has most power to move men, and especially uneducated men, to devotion; and therefore it speaks inaccurately of God and of events, seeing that its object is not to convince the reason, but to attract and lay hold of the imagination [ch. 6].

When scripture speaks plainly and rationally it mentions the fact that nature is unchangeable (Ps. 148:6; Jer. 31:35f.; Eccles. 1:10–12, 3:11).

Scripture is really intended to move the unruly wills of the stupid masses, and it serves its purpose when it keeps them under control. But philosophers who live according to reason must be free to understand nature as best they can. "Theology is not bound to serve reason, nor reason theology, but each has her own sphere" (ch. 15). Only for the irrational is scripture authoritative. Spinoza claims that his analysis is beneficial for the state, and will bring peace among people who are willing to be tolerant:

> Everyone should be free to choose for himself the foundations of his creed, and . . . faith should be judged only by its fruits. . . . This same liberty can and should be accorded with safety to the state and the magisterial authority—in fact . . . it cannot be withheld without great danger to peace and detriment to the community [ch. 1].

Since scripture no longer speaks authoritatively to us, there is no need for any kind of understanding of it but historical interpretation. "The meaning of scripture should be gathered from its own history, and not from the history of nature in general, which is the basis of philosophy" (ch. 15). The ultimate purpose of this study is the discovery of "universal truths expressly taught" (ch. 7). Thus scripture, when properly understood, will confirm the insights which reason has already attained by means of philosophy. The divorce of theology from philosophy results in the abandonment of theology by any intelligent person. We are to study scripture only for its historical interest, and we apply the ordinary rules of historical interpretation. In his seventh chapter Spinoza sets forth these rules.

First we examine "the nature and properties of the language in which the books of the Bible were written, and in which their authors were accustomed to speak." Since both Old and New Testament have Hebrew characteristics, when we understand the Hebrew idiom we can understand their manner of speaking. In the second place, we should analyze the subject matter of each book, arranging it under headings to show its contents. We should note the passages which are ambiguous or obscure or mutually contradictory. And finally, we must study the environment of the books. Who wrote them? What do we know of each author? "What was the occasion and epoch of his writing, whom did he write for, and in what language?" Then we examine the subsequent history of his book, and ultimately its inclusion in the canon.

Spinoza's method is very much like that followed in modern introductions to the books of the Bible. It is clear and rational. It avoids all the theological questions involved in the interpretation of scripture; for scripture has no authority over the interpreter's mind. It may govern his actions, but only if he is somewhat unintelligent. If he is truly rational, reason alone will guide his whole life. Spinoza's distrust of the authority of scripture or of the Church is more than equalled by his confidence in the powers of "impartial" reason, working without assumptions. He lives in the springtime of rationalism.

Spinoza was the most important advocate of the primacy of reason over scripture and the weight of traditional interpretation; but he had forerunners and allies, especially in the Netherlands. For instance, in 1658 a Unitarian physician named Zwicker had published his *Irenicum Irenicorum*, an attempt to bring warring Christians to admit that theology should be based first on reason and only secondarily on scripture and tradition. In an anonymous essay of 1683, *Miracles No Violations of the Laws of Nature*, it was argued that "most of the ancient fathers . . . and of the most learned theologues among the moderns" have held that the scriptures "aim only to excite pious affections in their breasts." A more moderate position was taken by Meyer, a Cartesian friend of Spinoza, who held in his *Philosophia sacrae scripturae interpres* (1666) that while scripture was the infallible word of God, it must be interpreted by reason; therefore things which appear unreasonable must be allegorized.[8]

Within the Roman church this attitude was also found in the critical work of Richard Simon (1638–1712). He had been a member of the Congregation of the Oratory, but left it in order to publish his *Histoire critique du Vieux Testament* (1678), in which he denied the Mosaic authorship of the Pentateuch, and his *Histoire critique du texte du Nouveau Testament* (1689). Both works were condemned by the Parliament of Paris; other writings of Simon were later attacked by Bossuet and Louis XIV.[9] In the English church a certain John Craig imitated his friend Newton's *Principia mathematica* in his *Theologiae christianae principia mathematica*. He held that since all evidence grows progressively less valid in the course of time, it should be possible to calculate the date when Christianity would cease to be credible. This date would be about the year 3144, and probably the second coming of Christ would take place then.[10]

In the first half of the eighteenth century rationalism achieved its greatest popularity. Countless pamphlets were written which expressed in popular form and language the arguments which philosophers had set forth several generations earlier. Thomas Woolston's *Discourses on Miracles* was the most influential; as a result of its publication sixty replies sprang into print, and Woolston was tried for blasphemy. In spite of his counsel's ingenious argument that he was simply returning to the allegorical method of the fathers, he was fined a hundred pounds. But by the middle of the century philosophy had found a new direction. Bishop Berkeley and William Law had demonstrated the invalidity of natural reason and shown man's need of revelation, and Hume had shown that skepticism could turn against reason itself. The conflicts over the interpretation of scripture gradually came to an end, at least in England. Rationalistic criticism of the Bible crossed the Atlantic to die in the arms of Tom Paine.

12

The Nineteenth Century

By the end of the eighteenth century the rational study of the Bible was developed to such an extent that hermeneutical handbooks setting forth the new method were in vogue. Such books were written by Ernesti and Semler and clearly show the growing interest in a purely historical understanding of scripture. Towards the end of the century Lessing, Herder, and Eichhorn composed historical analyses of the Bible which were highly influential for a generation. In the late eighteenth century the stage was set in Germany for the development of historical criticism.

Historical criticism of the Bible was not new; but it had usually been employed either by opponents of Christianity or by minority leaders within the church.[1] Now with the rise to importance of the German universities, the study of the Bible left the control of the church and moved to the somewhat secularized school.[2] This movement was like that in the twelfth century when biblical study was transferred from the cloister to the university; but the spiritual atmosphere of a nineteenth-century German university was very different from that of Paris, for example, in the Middle Ages. Above all, in the German university there was a new and romantic sense of freedom. Under the guidance of philosophy, especially that of Hegel, impartial objective research was to solve the riddles of history. The facts might be dissolved in source analysis; the all-important ideas would remain.

The relation of biblical interpretation to theology in the nineteenth century was very close. The critical historical method, which came to be regarded as the only legitimate kind of exegesis, at once guided theologians in their reconstructions of belief and provided a means of reorganizing the materials of theology found in the Bible. It was a compass and a pruning hook. Both Schleiermacher and Ritschl were proficient in New Testament criticism
110

and in systematic theology alike. And in the course of the century many critics came to regard criticism as identical with exegesis.

One of the most striking features of the development of biblical interpretation during the nineteenth century was the way in which philosophical presuppositions implicitly guided it. For most historical interpreters the rationalist attitude toward miracles was taken for granted. Later in the century the Hegelian distinction between external ideas and temporary forms was employed. And in the course of the century the differences between the biblical writings and any other writings came to be ignored. In large part, the idea of interpreting the Bible in the same way as any other book was popularized by Schleiermacher.[3]

The interpretative work of Schleiermacher represents the confluence of rationalism with the subjectivism of the Reformation. In his *Über die Religion* (1799) Schleiermacher rejected the absolute authority of scripture. "The holy books have become the Bible in virtue of their own power, but they do not forbid any other book from being or becoming a Bible in its turn." In fact, "the person of Jesus Christ, with all that flows immediately from it, is alone absolutely normative."[4] The mixing of rationalism with the spirit of the reformers is not altogether successful; for while much of Schleiermacher's New Testament criticism is acute,[5] in his posthumous *Leben Jesu* rationalism wholly wins the day. The resurrection of Jesus was his recovery from a lethargy; his ascension, his second and genuine death.

Schleiermacher's entirely rationalist contemporary, Paulus, asked, in his *Leben Jesu* (1828): "Has the fact narrated been produced, and how could it have been naturally produced?" For him the angels at the nativity were phosphorescence, the narratives of healings omit their natural causes, and the transfiguration story is the product of sleepy disciples who saw Jesus talking with two unknown persons during a beautiful sunset! A more critical and sounder analysis of the New Testament is to be found in the work of De Wette. His studies led him to a thorough skepticism concerning the possibility of answering many questions about the New Testament; there can be no life of Jesus; and our uncertainty ought to strengthen our faith.[6]

The most important New Testament critic of the nineteenth century was F. C. Baur, professor of historical theology at Tübingen from 1826 until his death in 1860.[7] Strongly under the influence of Hegel's theory of history, he and his followers believed in the dialectical development of dogma. Ideas came to their complete expression only gradually, through the setting forth of thesis, the opposition of antithesis, and the formulation of synthesis. Therefore the whole history of early Christianity was to be interpreted in the light of these ideas. The Judaizers present the thesis; they conflict with the antithetical Paul and his followers; finally gospels and epistles are written which synthesize both elements. Modern critics are often too scornful of Baur's analysis, and of Hegel. In many respects the Tübingen picture of early Christianity is distorted; but it is not basically incorrect. Baur founded a school of critics, some of whom were very able; but none was his equal. His most brilliant pupil was Ritschl, whose first book was strongly influenced by his teacher. The second work, *Die Entstehung der altkatholischen Kirche,* was a declaration of independence.

Another pupil of Baur, more famous than Ritschl, was D. F. Strauss, whose youthful *Leben Jesu* (1835) was very widely read. Indeed, when he was appointed professor at Zürich in 1839, a petition against him bearing forty thousand signatures caused the Swiss government to prevent his coming. For Strauss, Jesus was a wise man whom his ignorant contemporaries turned into a magician. We may wonder whether Strauss is entirely negative. He annihilates the traditional picture of Jesus and holds that we must believe in "the eternal Christ," the ideal of humanity as we conceive it in the nineteenth century.

We must not suppose that the "historical" interpretation of the Bible, especially in this somewhat erratic form, ruled unopposed even at Tübingen. A more influential teacher even there was J. T. Beck, who upheld the inspiration of the writers of scripture and the possibility of spiritual (pneumatic) exegesis.[8] He insisted that the Bible contained *Heilsgeschichte,* the "history of salvation" or of God's saving acts; it was therefore different from any other kind of history, and required different treatment. And there were many critics in other universities who refused to follow the radical school.

The influence of the radical school was very strong in Holland, where its skepticism, combined with philosophical determinism, shook the foundations of Dutch Protestantism.[9] As early as 1848 J. H. Scholten had distinguished, in his *Doctrine of the Reformed Church*, between the Bible and the Word of God contained in it. Appealing to scripture and to the reformers Scholten laid the foundations of a modernist theology based entirely on reason and conscience.[10] It was in Holland that the later Christ-myth theory flourished.[11]

In France the Tübingen school did not achieve great influence, and we find Renan not so much admiring the critics as wishing he had been born a free Protestant.[12] In general, moreover, the success of his own *Vie de Jésus* prevented Strauss's work from circulating widely. The Christ-myth theory had, moreover, originated in France, and its refutation had already been accomplished there. J. B. Pérès had used the methods of these scholars to 'prove' that Napoleon never lived.[13]

In England the influence of the critical school was most strongly felt by the broad-church group within the Anglican church. Coleridge, for example, was acquainted at least indirectly with the biblical criticism of Germany, and accepted its assumptions, though cautiously. In typical Anglican fashion he upheld the right of private interpretation, praised the traditional exegesis of the fathers and councils, and insisted on the necessity of scholarship.[14] His *Table Talk* is full of interesting comments on biblical questions.

The spirit as well as the method of the radical German school expresses itself in Coleridge: "Whatever may be thought of the genuineness or authority of any part of the book of Daniel, it makes no difference in my belief in Christianity; for Christianity is within a man."[15]

To a considerable extent he shares their attitude towards the miraculous, although he does not reject miracles. "In the miracles of Moses there is a remarkable intermingling of acts which we should nowadays call simply providential with such as we should still call miraculous."[16]

The old theories of inspiration are meaningless to him. "There may be dictation without inspiration, and inspiration without dictation; they have been and continue to be grievously confounded. Balaam and his ass were the passive organs of dictation; but no one, I suppose, will venture to call either of those worthies inspired. It is my profound conviction that St. John and St. Paul were divinely inspired; but I totally disbelieve the dictation of any one word, sentence or argument throughout their writings."[17]

Scripture must be interpreted by those who are spiritually competent to understand it. "Erasmus' paraphrase of the New Testament is clear and explanatory; but you cannot expect anything very deep from Erasmus. The only fit commentator on Paul was Luther—not by any means such a gentleman as the Apostle, but almost as great a genius."[18] Through the traditional English code of gentility shines a genuine appreciation of Luther's achievement.

The followers of Coleridge in the broad-church movement generally repeat his insights. Thus Thomas Arnold refers to the Bible as consisting of human writings and requiring a rational exegesis.[19] Similarly F. D. Maurice approved, at least tentatively, of biblical criticism—but only by those who were familiar with the ways of the Spirit. He taught that biblical inspiration was not "generically unlike that which God bestows on His children in this day." The Bible should not be set apart from life:

> Nothing is there taught as it is in the Koran, by mere decrees; everything by life and experiment.[20]

And yet, in the most famous trial of English biblical criticism in the nineteenth century, Maurice chose to use his influence against criticism. This was the case of Bishop Colenso.[21]

Colenso was an Anglican missionary bishop in Natal who endeavored not only to translate the Old Testament into the Zulu language, but also to explain some of the more obvious difficulties which occurred to his converts. A native assistant questioned the credibility of the story of Noah's ark and the justice of some of the Mosaic legislation on slavery. These questions started the bishop's own mind working, and he came to doubt the accuracy of biblical statistics. He could not any longer admit that six hundred thousand fighting men, plus women, children, and slaves, wandered in the desert of Sinai for forty years. And he came to admit many of the conclusions of continental scholars. While Colenso's case was eventually won in an English court, he suffered greatly from personal attacks and from the loss of Maurice's friendship.

Another unexpected opponent was the famous essayist Matthew Arnold, who blamed Colenso for lack of religious feeling. From one who was busily engaged in the work of refuting Baur and Strauss while at the same time reinterpreting a religion he did not really hold, this was a strange complaint. It will be worth our while to examine some of Arnold's observations on interpretation. His influence was extremely widespread in his day. In *Literature and Dogma, God and the Bible,* and *St. Paul and Protestantism* he presented himself as the cultivated layman's exegete. One of his fundamental points, though he does not use technical language, is his rejection of biblical inspiration in the traditional sense, and of miracle:

> The time has come when the minds of men no longer put as a matter of course the Bible-miracles in a class by themselves. Now, from the moment this time commences, from the moment that the comparative history of all miracles is a conception entertained and a study admitted, the conclusion is certain, the reign of the Bible-miracles is doomed.[22]

Like Cardinal Newman, Arnold regretted this development; unlike him, he did not have the assurance of faith to resist it.[23]

In spite of controversies, such as that just before Colenso over *Essays and Reviews* and that later over *Lux Mundi,* the critical movement continued to advance in the English Church, as well as among other Protestant bodies. Even Anglo-Catholics, who had begun with an ardent distrust of criticism and an enthusiasm for allegorism and the authoritative interpretation,[24] eventually valued the methods of criticism, especially as this group came to emphasize a rational theology. Criticism came to be respectable, even conventional. In the second quarter of the nineteenth century it had reached America, where it immediately flourished, especially in the universities of the Northeast. A few ecclesiastical trials gave added impetus to its growth. As early as 1829, a group of Anglican clergymen in New York translated from German and published a collection of "essays and dissertations in biblical literature." They were "well aware that there is a prejudice in some minds against German divinity and philology in general"; but they were determined to overcome it. More significant was the work of the

Congregationalists Moses Stuart and Edward Robinson of An-
dover. The latter when a professor at Union Theological Seminary
produced his monumental *Biblical Researches in Palestine, Mount
Sinai and Arabia Petraea* (1841). He had studied in Germany from
1826 to 1830.[25]

The end of the nineteenth century saw a certain stability enter
criticism in Germany. In England the phrase "assured results of
criticism" began to be used. This feeling of calm was due largely
to the work of two men, one in the Semitic and Old Testament
field, the other in New Testament and early Christian literature.
Both were enormously prolific and creative; both were regarded by
their followers as almost omniscient.

The Old Testament interpreter was Julius Wellhausen. The theory of origins named after him and after its founder, Graf, has
ruled Old Testament criticism almost down to our own day, and is
still held by many highly competent scholars. In brief, it is this:

> While a virtually unanimous tradition affirms the five books of Mo-
> ses to be the most ancient documents of Hebraic literature, and con-
> sequently to antedate the prophets, the school of Wellhausen puts off
> the solemn promulgation of the Law until after the Babylonian Exile
> and places the composition of the principal codes at the earliest after
> the great prophetical movement. Only the Book of the Covenant,
> and, possibly, the most ancient editing of the Yahwistic and Elohis-
> tic narrative sections could by this interpretation go back further than
> the eighth century. Instead of appearing as restorers of Mosaic mon-
> otheism, which the present order of the books of the Bible shows
> them to be, the prophets are represented as the first to build up and
> preach the idea.[26]

Many details of the Wellhausen theory have been altered by later
research, but it is possible that the reports of its death have been
exaggerated. But into the arena of present-day Old Testament criticism the author has no desire to enter.

For the New Testament the meaning of the nineteenth-century
critical movement is set forth in Harnack's *Das Wesen des Christentums* (The Essence of Christianity). This book consists of the
extemporaneous lectures which, at the height of his powers, the
great Berlin professor delivered to an audience of six hundred students. He appeals for the return of Protestantism to the religion of

Jesus which has been found behind the later ideas of Christology, ecclesiastical organization, and asceticism. Jesus' teaching can be analyzed under three heads:

> Firstly, the kingdom of God and its coming.
> Secondly, God the Father and the infinite value of the human soul.
> Thirdly, the higher righteousness and the commandment of love.[27]

The interpreter of the New Testament, in discerning these essential elements, is not reproducing the ancient message in its entirety. He cannot do so.

> There are only two possibilities here: either the Gospel is in all respects identical with its earliest form, in which case it came with its time and has departed with it; or else it contains something which under differing historical forms is of permanent validity.[28]

And—here Harnack is true to the spirit of the Reformation—each interpreter must decide this essence for himself. The Reformation rightly

> protested against all formal, external authority in religion; against the authority, therefore, of councils, priests, and the whole tradition of the church. That alone is to be authority which shows itself to be such within and effects a deliverance, the thing itself, therefore, the Gospel.[29]

Das Wesen des Christentums has often been criticized for separating Christ from the church, but Luther also appealed to Christ and the Gospel against the church of his day. Luther also simplified the Gospel. However, Harnack was not primarily a reformer. He claimed to be interpreting the teaching of Jesus as the essence of Christianity; and it is fairly evident that Jesus' teaching was more complex than the interpreters made it appear.[30] The New Testament itself, moreover, finds the center of the Christian religion in Jesus' resurrection, in the decisive act in which God entered history and vindicated his own purposes.

The nineteenth-century critical movement was not simply a movement in the history of interpretation, but (like every other exegetical school) had its own theological axes to grind. It stood for liberalism in theology. Any judgment on the work of the school must be made on the basis of this theological outlook as well as on the basis of the criticism itself. The two were closely connected. Today, after two wars we are less optimistic about the possibility of a Christian world, and after nearly a half-century of further criticism we begin to realize human potentialities for error and the limitations of the historical method. As pioneers the old critics cut down forests with abandon. The axe of criticism will be only one of the tools we employ.

13

Roman Catholic
Modernism

In spite of its professed stability, indeed immutability, the Roman church could hardly fail to be affected by the heavy seas of biblical criticism. In France, for example, though the church seemed to have weathered the gales of the Revolution and the Napoleonic wars, deep in the hold the dangerous water of liberalism was seeping through. And while eventually the ship's seams were caulked, and the water pumped overboard, for a time at least it appeared that there might arise a Catholicism which was also free. We need only mention the names of such Catholic leaders as Rosmini-Serbati, Döllinger, and Lord Acton, to imagine what might have been. And Newman, though as a convert hardly liberal-minded, gave at least the appearance of countenancing change.

Nevertheless the political leaders of Catholicism were able to prevent any such movement from developing, and the list of liberal writings placed on the Index steadily lengthened throughout the century. The *Syllabus errorum* and the declaration of papal infallibility in 1870 gave tremendous impetus to conservative forces within the church. And when to those documents we add the later encyclicals *Providentissimus Deus* (1893) and *Pascendi dominici gregis* (1907), it will be seen that the liberal hope was somewhat illusory. As Pius X pointed out in *Pascendi,* the plans of modernists were checked by three things: the scholastic philosophy, the authority of the fathers and of tradition, and the authority of the church.

To a Breton peasant boy studying for the priesthood in Paris in 1838, the crushing weight of these later authoritative decisions was naturally unknown. He was able to realize that he was being taught a "théologie des demoiselles" (a schoolgirls' theology), and he believed that it came from the past of Catholicism.[1] It did not represent the present or future. Similarly at Saint-Sulpice, as he says, "the Revolution had had no effect."[2] The Revolution came to the seminary as this boy, whose name was Ernest Renan, began his study of Hebrew.

At Saint-Sulpice he was brought into contact with the Bible and the sources of Christianity; and the ultimate result of his study was to overthrow what had been the foundations of his life. Eventually the problem was posed for him in this way:

> In a divine book everything is true, and since two contradictory statements cannot be true at the same time, there must be no contradictions in it. Now the attentive study that I made of the Bible, while revealing historical and aesthetic treasures to me, also proved to me that this book was no more exempt than any other ancient book from contradictions, mistakes, errors. In it there are fables, legends, traces of purely human composition.[3]

The idea came over Renan that in abandoning the church he might "remain faithful to Jesus," but eventually he gave up religion for rationalism. He could not accept the critical work of the Tübingen school, whose views he regarded as "exaggerated." But he could not remain a Catholic.

The tremendous popularity of his work, especially of his *Vie de Jésus,* increased the influence of the growing critical school in France. And the pontificate of Leo XIII, a great diplomat, gave the impression to some of the clergy, especially in France, that a compromise between Catholicism and biblical criticism would be possible.[4] The continual stream of condemnations of venturesome critics should have shown them their error;[5] but optimism was characteristic of the modernist movement.

Modernism was never a strongly organized or even a clearly defined movement. Instead, as Pius X described it in *Pascendi* it was a combination of all sorts of heresies. The only article of belief held by all its adherents was a faith in the spirit of the times and a rejection of immutability in doctrine. The protest of the modernists was centuries late. The edifice of Catholic dogma had been repaired by the Council of Trent and a pinnacle had been set on its peak by the declaration of papal infallibility. The authoritative interpretation of scripture had been reaffirmed against Protestants and "rationalists" alike, in *Providentissimus Deus* (November 18, 1893). The modernist cause, especially in the interpretation of scripture, was lost before the battle.

There were, of course, some reasons for their hopes of victory. In the first place, they were convinced that they represented the true mind of the church, and that the apologetic they were constructing was the only one which could carry Christian theology through the rough seas of modern science. In the second place, they were aware of the great acclaim which Newman's theory of development had won, and some of them—Loisy especially—believed that their own views were only extensions of Newman's thought. We can see that they must have misread Newman; but they did not think so. Finally, they had great confidence in the self-evident truth of science as an ally. They were rarely skeptical of the imposing edifice which nineteenth-century criticism had erected on the foundation of historical research. Loisy was always more confident of his own powers as an exegete than of the reliability of the materials with which he dealt. But such confidence was typical of the science of his day.

The culmination of modernist interpretation is to be found in Loisy's *The Gospel and the Church,* an immensely popular work which brought about his excommunication. It was intended to serve as a Catholic reply to Harnack's *Das Wesen des Christentums* (see p. 116). Rejecting the possibility of simplifying the Christian faith, he declares that

> we know Christ only by the tradition, across the tradition, and in the
> tradition of the primitive Christians. . . . The mere idea of the gospel
> without tradition is in flagrant contradiction with the facts submitted
> to criticism.[6]

Unfortunately he criticizes not only Harnack but also the official Catholic theory of the interpretation of scripture. He boldly explains away many New Testament passages as unhistorical, claiming that they are guaranteed by the church which invented them. And he clearly attacks the authoritative interpretation of the Bible:

> The work of traditional exegesis, from whence dogma may be said
> to proceed by a slow and continuous elaboration, seems in perma-

nent contradiction with the principles of a purely rational and historical interpretation. It is always taken for granted that the old Biblical
texts and the witness of tradition must contain the truth of the present time, and the truth is found there because it is put there.[7]

Loisy then criticizes the typological exegesis of the Old Testament
in the New, and the other "artifices of interpretation." Elsewhere
he distinguishes between historical and traditional interpretations:
"the first appertaining to them [the texts] by virtue of their origin
and true nature, the second that which has been grafted on to them
by the work of faith in the later evolution of Judaism and Christianity." Only the former should concern the critic.[8]

Loisy was searching for a way to reconcile the contradictions
between historical and theological exegesis. He had the misfortune
to work in a church where it was officially held that there are no
contradictions. His problem and his solution were misunderstood
and rejected. What had he tried to do? He had tried, so to speak,
to short-circuit criticism, to bypass it, while maintaining its complete validity in its own sphere. He came almost to proclaim a divorce between faith and knowledge.

It is interesting to observe that Loisy regarded his religious and
philosophical writing as of greater importance than his critical
work. In this he was probably right. As a historical critic he succeeded in being brilliant without being profound. His work often
lacks the depth that a more sympathetic understanding of early
Christianity would have given it. It is often merely ingenious. And
yet the problems which he posed, and for whose solution he sacrificed his Catholicism, still remain to disturb the theological world.
The relation between historical and spiritual exegesis has not been
settled.[9]

His withdrawal from the church took place before the inevitable
condemnation of errors which came in the decree of the Inquisition, *Lamentabili sane exitu* (July 3, 1907), and the encyclical
Pascendi dominici gregis (September 8, 1907). The decree lists
and condemns sixty-five propositions taken not only from the
works of Loisy but also from those of other modernists. But most
of the errors discussed concerned the New Testament, of which
Loisy had been a leading exegete. Among the exegetical views rejected were these: that the authority of the church cannot, even in

dogmatic definitions, determine the true meaning of scripture (prop. 4); that the deposit of faith contains only revealed truths and therefore the church cannot judge scientific work (prop. 5); that the exegete must forget the supernatural origin of the Bible and interpret it like other books (prop. 12); and that heterodox exegetes have been more accurate than Catholic ones (prop. 19). A more fundamental mistake, from the traditional viewpoint, was to hold that the inspiration of scripture did not prevent error in it (prop. 11). A proposition which really sums up the modernist attitude and reveals its fundamental incompatibility with the authoritarian Catholic point of view is this:

> No chapter of scripture from the beginning of Genesis to the end of Revelation contains a teaching absolutely identical with that which the Church sets forth on the same subject; and consequently no chapter of scripture has the same meaning for the critic as for the theologian [prop. 61].

The papal encyclical systematizes and perhaps unduly rationalizes the views of modernists. But not unfairly it attacks the double view of truth which they upheld. They said that as phenomena miracles and prophecies did not take place; these occurred only to the eye of faith:

> When they write history, they bring in no mention of the divinity of Christ; when preaching in churches they firmly profess it. . . . Hence they separate theological and pastoral exegesis from scientific and historical.

While the modernists claim to have no philosophy, actually their outlook is based on agnosticism, on what they call "the logic of facts." They distinguish between inner history and real history.[10] Building upon evolutionary theory, they arrange documents in accordance with it.

Fundamentally the objection to modernist teaching is based on the split which the modernists found between theology and science. The Thomistic view, as we have seen (chapter 9), does not contemplate the possibility of tension between reason and revelation, for reason provides the ground upon which the edifice of revelation is built. A purely objective interpretation of scripture, combined with a purely objective Aristotelian interpretation of nature, leads the way to Catholic theology. Other ways do not exist, or are heretical. As Pius X points out, the modernists should have been aware that their views had been condemned in advance at the Council of Trent and the Vatican Council of 1870.

There were several results of the papal condemnation. The Pontifical Institute of Biblical Studies was set up in Rome, and the Pontifical Biblical Commission, already appointed in 1901, was encouraged to publish its decisions. These decisions generally reaffirm the tradition of the church in questions of biblical criticism, but some of them are (it would seem) intentionally ambiguous. At any rate, Catholic critics have since taken advantage of certain ambiguities in order to claim a relative freedom for their studies.[11] The modernist crisis came to an end.

Half a century after *Providentissimus Deus,* Pius XII reiterated but reinterpreted its chief points in his encyclical *Divino afflante spiritu* (September 30, 1943). After tracing the progress in biblical studies encouraged by his predecessors, the Pope turns to the present state of exegesis and points out the achievements of modern learning. Biblical archaeology, papyrology, the discovery of more manuscripts, the study of ancient interpretation, and of ancient literary and oral style—each has made its contribution. But each has still more to give. The exegete must know the biblical language thoroughly. He must be expert in textual criticism, especially of the Greek and Hebrew texts. He must aim first at setting forth the literal sense of scripture, emphasizing its theological meaning; he must also stress the spiritual meaning built on the literal. And he must more vigorously study patristic exegesis.

What is the interpreter to do when he or she is confronted with the new questions and difficulties of our times? Above all he or she must consider the character of the writer of scripture. While the writer was inspired he did not lose his own personality, which we can come to know through the study of his times, his sources, his style. Ancient oriental writers have a way of writing quite unlike that of our times, and the exegete must try to return intellectually to these distant ages of the orient. Idioms, hyperboles, even paradoxes have their place in scripture. The exegete must determine what this place is. Many difficulties still remain in scripture, and comparatively few of them have been settled by the Fathers.

Biblical inerrancy must be maintained, as well as the doctrine of the church. But the Pope claims that a wide range of freedom is left for the Catholic exegete.

What were the ultimate results of the modernist crisis?[12] The optimistic prophets of modernism received a rude shock when condemnation succeeded condemnation and the movement apparently died. In any age the number of people actively concerned with the theory of biblical interpretation is small, and in an authoritarian community their needs are subordinated to the necessity of conformity. The decisions of the Biblical Commission, however, remained open to a measure of reinterpretation, as was shown conclusively in 1927. In 1897 the Holy Office had declared that the actually interpolated text of 1 John 5:7 ("there are three in heaven") was the genuine one; no Catholic critic could hold otherwise. Thirty years later, the crisis past, it could be stated that the earlier decision was intended only to curb the audacity of private teachers who took on themselves the right of judging the authenticity of the "comma" or interpolation. Actually Catholic writers may incline against the genuineness of the comma

> provided that they profess themselves ready to stand by the judgement of the Church, to which by Jesus Christ was entrusted the office not only of interpreting the sacred scriptures, but also of faithfully guarding them.

To non-Catholics this statement may seem somewhat equivocal. But, given the principle of authoritative interpretation, this is perhaps the only way in which development and change can be recognized. Catholics soon noted that *Divino afflante spiritu,* to use the words of the wartime *Revue biblique,*[13] opens a new era in the study of the holy scriptures. The years since have confirmed their conclusion.

14

Modern Protestant Interpretation

The University of Strasbourg in 1893 impressed a freshman student as not far from perfect. "Unhampered by tradition, teachers and students alike strove to realize the ideal of a modern university. There were hardly any professors of advanced age on the teaching staff."[1] The great liberal scholar H. J. Holtzmann lectured on the synoptic gospels, while the student could hear Windelband and T. Ziegler on the history of philosophy, Budde on the Old Testament, and Lobstein on dogmatic theology. Almost inevitably one would agree with the student that his teachers and their methods were the finest of the day. And yet, when the student, whose name was Albert Schweitzer, went on to investigate the synoptic gospels for himself, he came to doubt the fundamental principles of the liberal school.

Holtzmann had held that since the Gospel of Mark underlies both Matthew and Luke, Jesus can be understood from Mark alone. But when Schweitzer came to examine the tenth and eleventh chapters of Matthew, which mainly are not based on Mark, he could not deny their authenticity; for in them there is unfulfilled prophecy which is ascribed to Jesus. Why would the early church multiply difficulties for itself? Since it would not, these chapters, which reflect the idea of a supernatural, messianic world, must be substantially genuine. And the liberal picture of Jesus as simply an ethical teacher is shattered. Fortunately in the examination Holtzmann asked no questions bearing on this topic, and a debate was avoided. But Schweitzer knew that he had to continue his studies, taking advantage of the opportunity for independent scientific work which the German university of the day provided.

He went on to study at the Bibliothèque Nationale in Paris, and then spent the summer of 1899 in Berlin, where he heard lectures by the great scholars of the University. He was especially over-awed by Harnack. For two years he was a curate in Strasbourg while he obtained his licentiate in theology and in 1902 became a *Privat-dozent* at the University. Two faculty members protested against his appointment; they disapproved of his method of histori-cal investigation and feared he would confuse the students with his views. But thanks to Holtzmann's support he was appointed. In 1905 he gave a summer course on the history of research on the life of Jesus, and the resultant book, *Von Reimarus zu Wrede* (translated into English as *The Quest of the Historical Jesus*), was published the following year. In it Schweitzer pointed out that the principal scholars of the nineteenth century had held that Jesus' messiahship was simply ethical. Any apocalyptic elements in it were due to mistaken followers. On the other hand, it could not be denied that in the gospels there are eschatological elements. Those scholars who admitted this fact disposed of the evidence in two ways. Some (Colani, Volkmar, finally Wrede) denied that the es-chatology came from Jesus; a few (J. Weiss, Schweitzer himself) accepted its authenticity and took it to be the heart of the gospel.[2]

Schweitzer's work was remarkably influential. The liberal school had reached its height in Harnack's *Wesen des Christen-tums,* and fairly plainly had no further future. Christian theolo-gians and scholars were looking for a new prophet to lead New Testament interpretation out of the desert. And while Schweitzer's conclusions had largely been anticipated by Johannes Weiss, a popular study was needed in order to set them before the theologi-cal world. Like Loisy's *The Gospel and the Church* it attacked the liberal school at its weakest point, on historical grounds. In Eng-land it was warmly received, and the unhappy Tyrrell made use of it in his *Christianity at the Cross Roads.* It was of course at-tacked; Dean Inge found it "blasphemous." But the picture of Je-sus in terms of eschatology was not destined to fade; instead, as the twentieth century progressed, it grew more vivid. Schweitzer led a new school of interpreters into a new orthodoxy. But he him-self went to a medical mission in Africa.

Even before the coming of the First World War, students of the Bible had begun to realize the impossibility of explaining it by means of historical method as it was usually employed. Schweitzer himself was aware that every age has sought not a historical picture of Jesus, but a guide for life. And as the study of the Bible was developed after the war, it was demonstrated that the biblical narratives were never intended to be merely records. All the gospels, for example, were written to set forth Jesus as the Messiah and Son of God. They were written in faith to inspire faith. To the evangelists, questions of chronology, of fact as nineteenth-century critics regarded it, were not merely secondary; they were often irrelevant. And when their writings were examined by the same methods which had often been applied successfully to other ancient books, they could not be satisfactorily interpreted. No one can deny the genuine contributions which classical philology brings to the study of the Bible. But the books of the Bible were written in a believing community for believers; they are not "objective" history; indeed their authors would not be flattered to be called objective. These authors took a stand, and their decision colored every syllable of their writing. The quest of the 'Jesus of history' does not take us far behind the 'Christ of faith.'

Two conclusions can be drawn from this collapse of the older research into the life of Jesus. In the first place, it must be admitted that we know relatively little about his career. We do not know in what order events in his life took place. And it is impossible for us to attempt to draw a picture or diagram of his psychological development. Indeed, the attempt ought never to have been made; we do not possess the data for it; as E. Schwartz observed, the ancients were not interested in tracing character development.[3] Moreover, in the absence of such a picture we cannot have the boldness of nineteenth-century scholars in declaring sayings and incidents unauthentic. Jesus for us is not the "normal" person whom they hoped to find. And in the second place, since we cannot trace his human development we are confronted with his messianic character and have no alternative construction to substitute for it. Jesus in the gospels is presented to us as the Son of God. We can certainly distinguish among various interpretations of *Son of God*; but we cannot remove the idea from the gospels. They remain intransigently books of faith.

A result of the newer New Testament study has been renewed emphasis on the revelational quality of the New Testament and a decline in attempts to read the miraculous out of the original record. Miracle is deeply embedded in the gospel, and to omit it would take our gospels out of their first-century setting. The same change in emphasis has been felt in Old Testament study, where interest has centered on investigations in the theology of the Old Testament and in biblical archaeology.[4] A hypercritical literary criticism has tended to disappear.

The newer criticism of the scriptures is actually more skeptical than criticism in the nineteenth century, for it questions the possibility of knowing many things which were axiomatic then. Do we have sufficient information to determine whether such and such a passage is authentic or not? Often we do not, and a truthful criticism must admit its limitations. But it can accurately be said that nothing essential in the biblical record has been proved false, or indeed can be proved false. In any event the Christian's response to the record of revelation is never simply acknowledgment of fact. It is belief in and devotion to God. Faith is not to be placed in accounts of ancient events; faith is the Christian's relationship to God.

In the nineteenth and early twentieth centuries, critics laid great emphasis on the presumed objectivity of their studies. They tried to place biblical criticism among the sciences. But a cursory examination of the "assured results" of their investigations will show that they exaggerated their own objectivity. There always remains a subjective element which necessitates variety in exegesis. And the study of the art of interpretation reveals that a would-be "scientific" exegesis often robs the thing interpreted of most of its interest.

With these preliminary observations in mind, let us turn to consider the various developments within biblical interpretation in the early twentieth century, especially in the field of the New Testament.

There have been two principal elements in the New Testament study of this century. Both of them have been means by which the early church might be understood more clearly in terms of the actual historical setting in which it began. They have been methods for bridging the gap between the early church and the world, and for explaining its enigmas by comparison with other similar movements. The first method is that of the history of religions. During the last eighty years a great deal has been learned about the other religions of the Greco-Roman world, and much of the new material has seemed relevant to the understanding of early Christianity.[5] Unfortunately it is probably the case that we know less about ancient religion than the pioneers enthusiastically believed, and in any event many of the striking parallels can be explained as due to the influence of Christianity on its surroundings rather than vice versa. It was exciting to discover the resemblance between rebirth in the taurobolium and rebirth in baptism. But as conservative critics pointed out, the taurobolium was regarded as conferring eternal life only three centuries after Paul set forth his doctrine of dying and rising in baptism. Chronology was a hurdle which some of the pioneers (Frazer, for example, in *The Golden Bough*) failed to jump.

The other method also interprets the New Testament, especially the gospels, in relation to its environment. In this case the environment is the early Christian community and its oral transmission of tradition. The method, which deals with the oral circulation of the primitive tradition before the gospels were written, is called form criticism or form history, and attempts to explain the development of the forms within the tradition in terms of the community's needs.[6] The original oral tradition circulated in independent units which may be classified according to their forms. These forms include isolated sayings, which served as texts for early Christian preachers, parables, short stories for edification, and longer stories to satisfy the hearer's curiosity. Some form critics believe that the longer stories, betraying a more secular interest, are later in date than the shorter ones. All agree that the framework of the gospels, with its editorial transitions and careful juxtaposition of topics, is secondary. The evangelists were editors rather than authors.

This method is valuable in its emphasis on the *Sitz im Leben* (life situation) for every part of the tradition; but its importance may easily be exaggerated. Very often a saying of Jesus seems to fit perfectly into a situation after his death. But how do we know that such a situation did not exist in his lifetime? Often it is impossible to decide. And again, when Bultmann, for example, distinguishes sharply between Hellenistic and Jewish elements in the gospels, he neglects the extent to which Jewish thought, even in Palestine, was Hellenized. It should be pointed out that this method is not only critical but also theological. Bultmann, for example, employs it with a thorough skepticism in order to destroy the Jesus of history and insists on the necessity of the Christ of faith. While other form critics are not so doubtful of the possibility of historical knowledge, all agree that the tradition and the gospels which enshrine it came down in a believing community for the edification and instruction of believers. If by *the historical Jesus* we mean a man like us and of our own times whom we can find behind the tradition, our search is doomed to failure from the outset.[7]

On the other hand, many of Bultmann's disciples (and, to some degree, Bultmann himself) have become aware that the skepticism is not an integral part of the method, and in recent years they have been endeavoring to change their course, explaining the change as due to more adequate understanding of theological principles. The proclamation of the gospel is a proclamation of an act of God in time and space; therefore it must be possible to engage in a new quest of the historical Jesus. To one who has not accepted the fundamental principles, either historical or theological, of the school, it may be enough to suggest that neither the skepticism nor the theological explanation of the "new quest" is necessarily cogent. It may seem banal to hold that more was, or could have been, known about Jesus a few decades ago than some scholars said could be known. But such a tenet, based on a relatively commonsense approach to the gospels, at least spares one from having to hold that one is now permitted to look for the historical Jesus because the latest interpreters of the *kerygma* say that the search is necessary.

Indeed, it can be pointed out with H. Conzelmann that advocacy of a radical 'kerygmatic' approach has been largely confined to a small though influential group of German scholars who have postulated a sharp break between the Jesus of history and the Christ of faith. As he states, "most English theologians either do not react to form-criticism at all or acknowledge it merely as a formal classification of literary types and question whether any historical or systematic judgments can result from it." He himself recognizes that "an established continuity is in itself historically more probable than the assumption of a discontinuity which is hardly able to explain the formation of the categories of the community's belief."[8]

The real merit of form criticism—we should hold with the English theologians to whom Conzelmann refers—lies partly in its identification of preliterary forms and, more significantly, in its implicit recognition of the gospels as books of the church. They did not exist either prior to or apart from the church; like the church itself, they were created in response to the revelation of God in Jesus Christ; but the church, in and for which they were written, came into existence before they did.

Another method, closely allied to these two, is the environmental study of the New Testament, in which the social situation at the time of Jesus or of the apostles is carefully analyzed and the accounts of their sayings and doings analyzed in the light of the environment. Certain critics, indeed, claim that this method can be applied "rigidly"; but the rigidity will come from them rather than from the materials of their study. Even the Dead Sea Scrolls may not reflect *the* Jewish background of Jesus and his disciples. A similar observation applies to the Greco-Roman world of the time. To be sure, many distinctions can be made; but how is one to explain the fact that certain critics regard the Fourth Gospel as a completely Greek book, while some rabbinic scholars hear echoes of Jewish thought all the way through it? Rigidity is not even a suitable goal for methods of biblical interpretation, much less an achievement.

These two methods, the study of early Christianity with other religions and the study of traditional forms, have made contributions to our understanding of scripture. Perhaps the results are not so impressive as the technicians have claimed. Doubtless the study of early Christianity in the light of apocalyptic Judaism, which it presupposes, will have much to offer us. But unless the New Testament is studied as a product of Christian faith, it is lifeless. It is itself not objective, and it was never meant to be studied objectively. For this reason the revival of biblical theology in the forties and fifties was important. It treated the Bible like any other book but went on to study the things which the biblical authors consider essential. It did not seek information which the Bible did not intend to give. And while our theological interests are not identical

with those of the first century or the second, our studies gain renewed vigor when we treat the record of the biblical revelation as
a book of God's ways with humans. It is not simply a record of
"facts." And in awareness of the nature of the Bible, modern biblical study can go on to new achievements and discoveries.

Here we may mention the prophet of biblical theology in our
times: Karl Barth.[9] No one did more to recover the authority of
the Bible for our day. By rigorously contrasting the Word of God
with the word of man, by insisting on the chasm between the Creator and his creation, Barth restored the Bible to its place of honor
in the structure of Christian faith. If at times he exaggerated the
impotence of human reason, his exaggeration was a salutary corrective to the somewhat jejune liberalism of early twentieth-cen-
tury exegesis. His thought took us back to the spirit of the reformers.

As a man of the twentieth century, he accepted whatever of
value the nineteenth century offered, and made it his own. At the
same time he reminded us to recognize that God speaks to us in
the Bible. On the one hand:

> The Bible is the literary monument of an ancient racial religion and
> of a Hellenistic cultus religion of the Near East. A human document
> like any other, it can lay no *a priori* dogmatic claim to special atten-
> tion and consideration.[10]

But it is also a book of God.

> He it is of whom the Bible speaks. And is he spoken of elsewhere?
> Certainly. But whereas elsewhere consideration of him is left to the
> last, an imposing background, an esoteric secret, and therefore only
> a possibility, in the Bible he is the first consideration, the fore-
> ground, the revelation, the one all-dominating theme.[11]

It may well be the case that Barth paid inadequate attention to
historical and philological study. Future interpreters will doubtless
go beyond his thought in these directions. Certainly he failed to
make the Bible fully comprehensible in relation either to ancient or
to modern culture. But he did not regard these comments as criticisms, and anyone who interprets the Bible after him has to take
into account the tremendous theocentric concern which governed
his thought.

15

The Interpretation of
the Bible

Many years ago, when the first edition of this book was published, it seemed much easier to say something about the contemporary scene and to make predictions about the future than it seems today. In part, the change in my mind is due to further study; in part it is due to what can be regarded either as a blurring of lines formerly distinct or as a movement toward a more positive and unified kind of interpretation. In a review of the first edition the late Joachim Wach suggested that it was not clear whether I was studying the methods actually employed by the interpreters or examining the theories of hermeneutics which they were following. I now despair of making this distinction, since in most of the patristic writings I have read the methods are similar to the theories but are by no means identical. Indeed, I am not entirely certain that a detailed hermeneutical system is either possible or desirable. Wach went on to say that "if we want hermeneutics we shall have to articulate clearly the theological principles upon which it will have to be constructed." This means that we have to enter what Bultmann calls the "exegetical circle" in which theology, somehow based upon the Bible, informs the hermeneutical method, which in turn makes interpretation of the Bible possible for theology. To a considerable degree this circle has been present and is present in the minds of interpreters of the Bible. But I should now ask whether or not theology is, or should be, based entirely or exclusively upon the Bible; and if (as I should hold) it is not so based, but is also informed by tradition and reason, then the circle no longer retains its perfect circularity.

It would appear that the primary task of modern interpreters is historical, in the sense that what they are endeavoring to discover is what the texts and contexts they are interpreting meant to their authors in their relationships with their readers. The work begins with philology. They must first examine the text of the documents which they are studying, in order to find out how the texts were transmitted and what the process of transmission involves in relation to the original document, no longer extant. Second, they must consider the literary form of the documents and the forms employed within it; they must take into account the language and style which its author used. Third, they must bear in mind the historical setting in which the author wrote what he wrote. For the New Testament, this setting is a triple one: (*a*) it is the Greco-Roman world, with all its variety, at the beginning of our era; (*b*) it is a world more or less closely related to Judaism, with all its variety; and (*c*) it is the community of the early Christian church, in which variety was also present. Similarly with regard to the Old Testament the historical setting is not simply the ancient Near East at various periods of time; it is also Israel as a community of faith, worship, and behavior, with all the variety present therein.

This is to say that environmental study is not a simple matter of coordinating the Old Testament or the New with the non-Israelite or non-Christian cultures in which Israel and the church found themselves. It is also, and more important, a matter of coordinating the literature with the life of the community out of which it came and for which it was written. One might even speak of Israel or the church as the hypotheses which alone make the Old and New Testaments comprehensible. Without Israel, no Old Testament; without the church, no New Testament.

At the same time, one cannot treat everything in either Testament as a permanently valid expression of the life of Israel or of the church. Both Israel and the church were historically conditioned in various ways by their non-Israelite, non-Christian environments, and one function of historical interpretation is to see the extent to which the influence of the environment has affected various writings or various parts of writings.

Having entered this *caveat,* one can now proceed to take a farther step—in the direction of theological interpretation. The Bible, after all, is not read simply because of the information it conveys about ancient Israel or the early church. It is read because people believe that in it they find expressed something of God's acts and intentions and demands. Why do they hold this belief? In my opinion, they hold it (*a*) more generally, because they find that the words of the Bible speak directly to them, just as they did to the people of ancient times (in other words, the human situation provides continuity between ancient people and ourselves), or (*b*) more specifically, because they recognize the continuity of the church now and the church then. The first kind of presupposition is maintained by the more individualistic kind of reader; the second, by the more corporate- or community-minded. The second is more congruent with the idea we have already expressed, that is, that the hypothesis of the church is necessary in order to make historical sense of the biblical documents.

It can be argued, of course, that there is no real continuity between the church now and the church then. Usually this argument is accompanied by a theory of the decline and fall of the early church, and of the restoration or new creation of the true church at some later date. Such a theory, however, usually neglects the extent to which the elements characteristic of the decline are to be found in the New Testament, and it assumes that the church as restored or freshly created is exempt from outside environmental influences. For these reasons decline-and-fall theories are hard to substantiate.

On the other hand, there are obvious differences between the church now and the church then. There is a difference between the apostolic church and the church of the third century, as Cyprian stated, followed by the Reformers and by the great historians of the nineteenth century. There are differences between the apostolic church and the church in every succeeding period, whether these differences are explained as due to decline or to development or to constant adaptation to various environments.

This means that the continuity between the church now and the church then is not equivalent to identity, as if a member of the church now were automatically provided with a guarantee of correct biblical interpretation. Members of the present church stand at this end of the long history of biblical interpretation, and in it they can see not only the various ways in which the Bible has been interpreted but also something of the extent to which the interpretations have been conditioned by the church's past circumstances.

They may find meaningful Calvin's emphasis on the "internal witness of the Holy Spirit," but they will recognize that in various circumstances the Spirit has had different emphases in what he said to the churches.

But in spite of the diversity in biblical interpretation there is also a measure of unity. This unity is provided by the church's emphasis upon tradition, a tradition itself flexible but ultimately derived from the apostolic age. The tradition is expressed primarily in (a) credal forms and (b) liturgy. The creeds of the church have varied, as far as details are concerned, but they maintain continuity with such New Testament statements as "for us there is one God the Father . . . and one Lord Jesus Christ" (1 Cor. 8:6). The liturgies of the church have varied too, but in general they maintain continuity with the baptism and the Lord's Supper of the apostolic communities. The creeds represent the continuing church's judgments as to the essential theological content of the Bible; the liturgies provide the contexts in which the religious meaning of biblical passages is to be understood. This is not to say that individual students of the Bible cannot attain to fresh insights into the meaning of the texts; it is to say that their insights should be checked with the interpretations implied by the context of the church, which is (with the qualifications noted above) the context within which the texts were written.

Is biblical interpretation scientific? Such a question, it would appear, has to be answered both no and yes. It is not scientific in the sense that an observer free from presuppositions and prejudices can simply analyze the biblical texts and produce a startling new and true hypothesis to explain them. Such a hypothesis could hardly be new, in view of the multiplicity of hypotheses produced in the last two hundred years or so; it could hardly be true, in view of the shakiness of such hypotheses when their fundamental bases are questioned. For example, New Testament critics have often noticed that in the gospels there are two views of the coming of the Kingdom of God. According to the one, it is entirely future but imminent; according to the other, it is in part present in the ministry of Jesus. One could proceed to regard these views either as complementary or as mutually exclusive. If they are mutually exclusive, only one of them represents the view of Jesus. Very generally speaking, the early church believed that the Kingdom was in part present in Jesus' ministry. Therefore the view that the Kingdom was coming immediately was held by Jesus. The presupposition here is that the church, faced by the nonfulfillment of Jesus' predictions, reinterpreted his message and thus distorted it. But if the church was so anxious to reinterpret, why do we find futurist passages in the gospels at all? The church's forgers must have been singularly halfhearted and inept. The view that Jesus proclaimed nothing but the future coming of the Kingdom (a) is based on a refusal to treat his sayings as complementary, and (b) results in a highly unconvincing picture of the work of those who transmitted and recorded his words.

This is not to say that he spoke every word recorded in exactly the way in which the evangelists have written it down. It is merely to say that a purely analytical method, looking for or even creating inconsistencies, cannot adequately interpret the Bible which reflects the unity-in-diversity of the church.

On the other hand, biblical criticism is scientific in the sense that it involves analysis before and alongside the synthesis towards which it aims. There is variety in the ways in which the church proclaimed the gospel and in the ways in which its members worked out the gospel's implications. This variety can be explained, at least in part, in relation to the various historical circumstances involved. In addition, before students reach the level of historical analysis they have to engage in the relatively scientific operations of textual and literary criticism.

Textual criticism, rarely practiced in the ancient church in adequate fashion, consists of (a) the collection and comparison of the ancient manuscripts, versions, and citations and (b) the attempt to provide an explanation of agreements and disagreements; the goal of the method is the recovery of the earliest and/or most nearly authentic readings of the texts. In recent times important discoveries of textual materials have been made—for the Old Testament, among the Dead Sea Scrolls; for the New Testament, among papyri found in Egypt. These discoveries have moved our access to the textual tradition back about a millennium for the Old Testament and to the second and third centuries for the New. In addition, some progress has been made in regard to theory. Previously textual study of the Bible was based on the model of classical philology, a realm in which the paucity of manuscripts made possible a genealogical approach. The "descent of manuscripts" could be traced. In dealing with the Bible, however, the abundance of materials and the extent of textual corruption means that family relationships are much less significant. There are text types but few "families." This discovery may well mean that the recovery of the original authentic text, at points where disagreements exist, has become an 'impossible possibility'.

Literary criticism is a mixture of the unscientific and the scientific. It is scientific when it is concerned with the style and vocabulary of the author under consideration. Style and vocabulary can be understood by means of careful examination of the documents, and this understanding leads directly to awareness of what the author intended to say and the way in which he said it. In recent times, biblical interpreters have rightly paid much more attention to this question than to such matters as the date and authorship of the various writings. Indeed, the latter questions belong to historical criticism rather than to literary analysis. And historical criticism comes after literary study, not before it. In order to set a literary phenomenon, such as a book of the Bible, in its historical context, one must first know what the phenomenon is—as literature. Before dealing with the presumed sources of one of the gospels, the student must acquire some awareness of the evangelist's style and vocabulary. He must learn how the evangelist expresses his ideas. A similar observation may be made in regard to the Pauline epistles. The first task of the interpreter is to try to discover what Paul said and how he said it (textual and literary criticism). Only after providing this kind of analysis can the interpreter proceed to ask why he said it.

It is at this point that biblical interpretation passes beyond what may be regarded as relatively scientific and enters the areas of history and theology. Interpreters as historians look not only at the documents but also at the situations behind the documents and contemporary with them. For instance, in the Old Testament they are concerned both with the patriarchal legends as reflections of very early times and with the significance of these legends for those who transmitted and recorded them. Interpreters ask not only how they were handed down but also why they were handed down. In the New Testament they seek to find the common core of preaching and teaching which lies behind the various documents, though they do not or, at any rate, should not try to press unity into uniformity.

In addition to looking for those factors which bind the biblical books together, the interpreter is engaged in discovering the relation of the books to the various environments in which they were written. The primary environments of the Bible, as we have suggested, are Israel and the New Israel, the church. But neither the Old Israel nor the New has existed in a historical vacuum. As known historically, the church is the visible church, proclaiming its gospel and living its life in various cultures, influencing these cultures and being influenced by them. The apostle Paul himself stated that he "became all things to all men" in the service of the gospel (1 Cor. 9:19-23). One purpose of environmental study is to see the manner and the extent to which the gospel was modified as it was thus presented. This purpose is both historical and theological. It is historical insofar as the interpreter is concerned with the history of the modifications in relation to (a) the history of the church and (b) the history of culture—in this instance, the culture of the Roman world and of Judaism. It is theological insofar as the interpreter discovers the Christian gospel which underlies the various modifications and, modified or unmodified, remains significant today.

Here interpreters run considerable risk of error. They can hardly avoid the influence of historical judgments upon their theological conceptions and that of theological concerns upon their historical ideas. All they can hope for is that they can work relatively freely and adequately in both areas. In regard to history, they can try to avoid the conventional clichés which turn events into static stereotypes. Some of these clichés have been attacked in an admirable study by James Barr, *The Semantics of Biblical Language* (1960), especially the verbal contrast between *Hebrew* and *Greek*. Others remain on the scene, with varying degrees of potency. *Prophet* and *priest, faith* and *moralism, authentic* and *redactional*—all reflect the petrified determination of our predecessors to express its theology in pseudohistorical terms. This is to say that bad theology and bad history work together.

Similarly, the notion that the proclamation of Jesus was strictly futuristic seems to be related to theological concerns. If one is going to obliterate the history of the church after the first century, one does well to maintain that Jesus never envisaged the possibility of the continuation of its life. On this basis the history of the church becomes the history of a mistake. Baptism was borrowed from John the Baptist and Paul's interpretation of it as dying and rising with Christ came from the Greco-Roman mystery religions. The Lord's Supper cannot be based upon the Last Supper, for the gospel account of the latter is an etiological cult legend. Jesus had disciples, certainly, but the notion that there were twelve of them, or that they were called apostles, is due to the creative imagination of the very institution which he did not found.

This kind of interpretation does not seem to leave much of the New Testament standing, and it suggests that the early church, almost completely discontinuous with Jesus, consisted of nothing but wildly creative syncretists. Perhaps there was a Jesus of history, but if there was, any historical image of him was suppressed and/or distorted in favor of the Christ of faith. Here the work of the newer German critics, ably interpreted by James M. Robinson (*A New Quest of the Historical Jesus,* 1959), plays a significant part. First, it is obvious that the early church is not absolutely continuous or identical with the community of disciples before the resurrection. Christians themselves were aware that something new had taken place. Indeed, "newness of life" is one of the primary consequences of the resurrection. There were also new directions: Paul speaks of Jesus as "the minister of the circumcision" (Rom. 15:8) and of himself as the one sent, in consequence of the resurrection, to proclaim Christ among the gentiles (Gal. 1:16). But second (and equally important), it is obvious that the early church remained continuous with the preresurrection disciples. Paul himself speaks of the "twelve" (1 Cor. 15:5); he knows traditions which come from Jesus. Above all, the center of the Christian proclamation continues to lie in Jesus, in his deeds and in his words. Some knowledge about Jesus was and is indispensable for the existence of the proclamation. For this reason the quest of the historical Jesus, not absolutely new but reflecting new concerns, continues. Among its most prominent advocates we may mention W. G. Kümmel (*Prophecy and Fulfilment,* 1957) and G. Bornkamm (*Jesus of Nazareth,* 1960).

In the earlier edition of this book I sought to bridge the gap between historical and theological understanding of the Bible by emphasizing the subjectivity present in exegesis and by claiming that there are meanings present within the texts which become clear, or clearer, only in the light of later experience in the life of the church. Today it hardly seems necessary to insist upon the ubiquity of subjectivity. Indeed, it may be suggested that subjectivity has been overemphasized and that the interpreter owes a measure of objectivity to the document with which he deals. In the language of Buber, he does not treat the document or its author as an It but as a Thou, a Thou which speaks to him as he enters into the exegetical conversation. The Thou has rights over against the subjectivity of the interpreter. As for the varying meanings which texts acquire in the history of interpretation, the situation in which variety emerges is no different from what we find in relation to any literary phenomena or any historical phenomena. There is no one fixed meaning of the works of Homer or Virgil or Shakespeare. The meanings vary in relation to the historical circumstances of the readers. Similarly, the Roman Forum meant one thing to first-century Romans, another to Atilla, another to the eighteenth-century English, another to any one of us. The notion that there is a single meaning can be labelled as "misplaced concretion."

The problem today is not so much how to allow for variety as it is to suggest limits. Does a biblical text convey at least a central meaning or cluster of meanings? In generations recently past it has been supposed that the primary meaning could be recovered by setting a text in its historical environment, to and in which it spoke univocally. This supposition led to what has been called parallelomania, the collection of parallels both Jewish and Greek, in the belief that the meaning of a text could be explained as identical, or practically identical, with the meaning of a parallel. This belief is false, since parallel texts are often written for purposes quite different from each other. It is the context which counts. And in the case of New Testament texts, the context must be supposed to be the Christian church; for it was the church in which and for which the texts were written, by members of the church; it was the church which preserved, selected, and transmitted the texts. The central meaning or cluster of meanings is therefore to be found within the church's life and understanding, broadly considered. This means that the interpreter's awareness of the church, both ancient and modern, cannot be limited, superficial, or one-sided. It must be, in the best sense of the word, catholic. It cannot be so narrow as to lay emphasis solely on the synoptic gospels at the expense of John, on the major Pauline epistles at the expense of the pastorals or Hebrews, or on Paul at the expense of James. One-sided emphases of this kind, like the pseudohistorical antitheses previously mentioned, result in inadequate theological and historical interpretations of the New Testament, just as exaggeration of the prophetic as against the priestly led to poor Old Testament exegesis.

In arguing for a "catholic" interpretation of the Bible, it will be seen, we have tried to uphold the essential validity of the principles set forth by such early writers as Irenaeus, Tertullian, and Augustine (see chapter 8). We have done so primarily on the ground that the Church provides the essential historical-theological context in which the meaning of the Bible becomes clear. Another line of argument has been emphasized in recent years, perhaps especially in the writings of J. Daniélou. This argument is based on the historical function of tradition. Modern study has shown that many of the books of the Old Testament and the New alike represent the deposit of oral tradition. The tradition handed down in and by the community is therefore prior to the written form in which it is now available. Yet from external evidence we know that the community continued to exist; it did not come to an end when the tradition was crystallized in writing. Therefore the tradition is both prior and posterior to its written formulation, and it is just as important as scripture is, as a witness to the nature of the church's faith and life. To put the point another way, scripture is nothing but the written expression of tradition.

The line of argument can be confirmed by considering the question of the New Testament canon. It does not seem correct in any way to claim that the Bible (Old or New Testament or both) brought the Church into existence. Both Bible and church are at once acts of God and men's responses to acts of God—the New Testament most clearly to God's act in Christ or, in more traditional terminology, the Incarnation. Of the two, however, the church is the prior. And the church exercised some kind of collective judgment in selecting certain books to constitute the New Testament and in excluding others. It was over a long period of time that the church made up its mind to accept such documents as Hebrews, all seven of the Catholic Epistles, and Revelation, and to exclude some of the writings of the apostolic fathers from the canon. It can, however, be argued with O. Cullmann that the final decision is not reversible. But one must remember that this "final" decision was not the product of a first- or second-century decision or of the work of a council; it came very gradually, and general agreement was reached only in the fourth and fifth centuries. This is to say that the canon as we know it is no earlier than the creeds, the earlier councils, and the developed ministry and theology of the ancient church.

The canon as it stands is the product of a process like the development of the church or of doctrine. One cannot absolutize a canon within the canon any more than a church within the church (equals a sect) or a doctrine within the body of Christian doctrine (equals heresy). Certainly individuals or groups can find certain books or aspects of church or doctrine more meaningful than others, but this weight of emphasis does not create a license to reject or deny the rights of others, living or dead. Moreover any rigid application of external criteria, as if philosophical or other standards could judge scripture, cannot be tolerated. In either case there are no absolutes. The canon itself is not a weapon for defending territory or extending gains.

When the reformers found a great gulf fixed between the scriptures and the rest of Christian literature, their discovery was at least partly due to (a) their unhistorical view of church history and to (b) the loss of the documents of the second century which bind together the New Testament with the more highly developed Christian writings of the third and fourth centuries. The reformers did not know most of the writings of the apostolic fathers or any of the genuine writings of the apologists. They knew the Old Testament Apocrypha but were unwilling to use these documents in relation to the New Testament background. For them the New Testament had practically no historical context.

Today, however, the situation is quite different. A great deal of light has been cast upon the background of the New Testament not only by intensive study of the Greco-Roman world, of Judaism (both Hellenistic and rabbinic), and of early Christianity as seen both inside and outside the New Testament, but also by the discovery of the Dead Sea Scrolls (beginning in 1947) and of the Gnostic library at Nag Hammadi in Egypt (including a complete aprocryphal gospel, that of Thomas). These discoveries, not yet fully assessed, have necessitated renewed emphasis on the historical context of the Bible, especially the New Testament.

At the same time, the problem of theological interpretation, even within the context of the church, has continued to be acute. For more than a generation the question of "demythologizing," brought to the fore by Rudolf Bultmann, was considered central by many. Modern people, thinking in the terms of modern science or scientific philosophy, no longer believe in a "three-story universe" or in apocalyptic eschatology or in miracles. Therefore it is the duty of the interpreter to take the insights of the Bible which are expressed in mythical language (language related to such matters as ancient cosmology, and so on) and reinterpret them in a language relevant to moderns. The novelty present in demythologizing does not seem to lie in its criticism of the ancient worldview, for such criticism has been vigorously expressed by critics since Spinoza's time (see chapter 11) and, indeed, was expressed by ancient men themselves—for example, Origen (see chapter 6). The novelty lies in the thoroughness with which an effort is made to separate the primary elements in the Bible from the secondary, and to reinterpret what is regarded as primary in terms of existentialist philosophy. The original and authentic work of the evangelist John thus becomes an existential proclamation, spoiled by disarrangements and by additions made by an 'ecclesiastical redactor'.

The trouble with this kind of interpretation, in my opinion, is twofold. First, it is assumed that there was a single ancient worldview which can be reinterpreted wherever it appears in the New Testament; similarly, it is assumed that there is a single modern world-view and that this world view is correct. Second, the biblical texts undergo a kind of metamorphosis as their more obvious historical meaning is transmuted into something more closely resembling the intention of the existentialist exegete. To some extent both difficulties are genuine. There are passages in the Bible which reflect historical conditioning more than the central proclamation of the gospel (1 Cor. 11:3–16 may serve as an example)—though we must remember that all the passages are historically conditioned. It is also the case, as we have already said, that there is no single, absolutely final interpretation which completely exhausts the potentialities of most biblical passages. But the major difficulty which arises out of demythologizing is that it tries to force on the passages more than they will bear, or should be expected to bear. The Bible is not the sole source of Christian theology, though it may be a primary one. We repeat the quotation from Richard Hooker:

> As incredible praises given to men do often abate and impair the credit of the deserved commendation, so we must likewise take great heed lest by attributing to scripture more than it can have, the incredibility of that do cause even those things which it hath abundantly to be less reverently esteemed.

The locus of demythologizing, then, lies not in biblical exegesis but in the systematic theology of the church, of which biblical theology is only a part.

To a considerable extent we should regard the modern endeavor to construct "biblical theology" as related to the task of demythologizing. Biblical theology is important insofar as it represents an attempt to systematize the "detached insights" of the biblical writers and to find the central focus or foci of their thought. But biblical theology, even when successfully reconstructed, is not a substitute for Christian theology, the product of many centuries of Christian thinking. Biblical theology can supply norms apart from which the church cannot remain Christian, but these norms do not constitute the whole of theology.

There is a sense in which scripture speaks to the reader more di-

rectly than does any other Christian literature. In part this direct-
ness is due to the closeness of prophets and apostles to the acts of
God to which they bear witness. It is also due to the fact that the
church has recognized that this collection of writings somehow
bears the imprint of the Spirit. And it is in this regard that we
agree with Bultmann that a "prior understanding" is a necessary
prerequisite for the interpreter of the Bible.[1] According to Bultmann, if man's existence "were not motivated (whether consciously or *unawares*) by the inquiry about God in the sense of the
Augustinian *'Tu nos fecisti ad Te, et cor nostrum inquietum est,
donec requiescat in Te,'* then neither would he know God as God
in any manifestation of Him." In our view, Bultmann's "unawares" and "consciously" correspond to (*a*) the general recognition
of the continuity of human situations and (*b*) the more specific recognition of the continuity of the life of the church. Thus while it is
possible for a non-Christian reader of the New Testament to obtain
genuine insights into its meaning, the more specific understanding
which comes from recognizing it as the book of the church can be
reached only through participation in the church's life. This, it
seems to me, is the real "prior understanding" which is necessary.
At the same time, I should hesitate to say that the Bible can be understood and interpreted only by Christians, especially since modern study owes much to great Jewish and secularist exegetes. It
would be better to maintain that both roads to understanding, that
through humanity in general and that through Christianity in particular, must be kept open. The Christian exegete is responsible for
remembering that above both Bible and church stands the God to
whom both point; the non-Christian exegete must remember the
community for which the Bible was created. Both must recall the
words with which Bultmann's essay concludes:

> The exegete is to "interpret" Scripture after he has responsibly
> "heard" what Scripture has to say! And how is he to "hear" without
> *understanding?* The problem of interpretation is precisely that of
> understanding.

One can agree with this statement, provided that he continues to
bear in mind the danger latent in the word *understanding.* If this
means that I cannot "understand" the Bible unless I rewrite it using

my own categories, I am then replacing both Bible and church by these categories, and ultimately I am creating God in my own image. This is of course the danger present in all theological systems and especially in those where the allegorical method, or its modern equivalents, is present. (Daniélou has pointed out some analogies between demythologizing and Origen's allegorizing.) Interpretation can become so devoted to understanding in modern terms that it neglects Barth's emphasis upon the strangeness of the Bible. The apostle Paul was not averse to using analogical language and metaphors drawn from contemporary thought, but at one point he insisted upon the limits of "modern" categories. He could argue about death and resurrection by using comparisons with natural phenomena (though he did not regard them as simply natural), but he could not stop with such analogies:

> Though Jews seek signs and
>   Greeks seek wisdom,
>   we proclaim Christ crucified:
>   to Jews a stumbling block,
>   to gentiles foolishness—but
>   to those who have been called,
>   both Jews and Greeks,
> Christ the power of God and the wisdom of God.

PART 2

Preface
to Part 2

Here the "short history" really ends. In the second edition of 1963 as in the first edition of 1948 there were a few nods toward prophecy and theoretical considerations. For this edition the predictions of 1963 seem almost as outmoded as those made earlier. My basic purpose, after all, was to tell about the past. I certainly do not claim complete objectivity for my version of the story, but on the other hand I do not think I distorted it greatly. Twenty years or so studying the Gnostics have not raised the grade I should give them as exegetes. "Creativity" does not always atone for perversity.

The book was thus what we may call open-ended. In other words, it was a history in search of an explicitly philosophical or theological conclusion or at least able to accept one. And since much modern scholarship in biblical interpretation is devoted to methods and inferences rather than to the ancient texts in their own interrelations, it seemed good now to apply to a theologian in order to see what systematic insights might emerge from his contemplation of my text.

David Tracy, my colleague in the Divinity School of the University of Chicago, was the inevitable candidate. He and I had jointly taught a course on the New Testament canon and had been surprised to discover how complementary our ideas were. He assured me that he found almost everything in the book sympathetic though he did not specify areas of disagreement, nor did I. There is some basis for the compatibility. Both Tracy and I take seriously our responsibilities to the Roman Catholic and Anglican churches, while both of us take great pleasure in teaching in a highly stimulating interdenominational divinity school. He therefore makes an admirable continuator and interpreter of the book.

This is not to say, however, that his is the only ending that

151

could be provided. Indeed, his ending with its emphasis on the most modern interpretation suggests a useful way to read the book. The reader could study both parts and then produce his or her own ending for the tale. A more individualistic reader (e.g., a Gnostic) might thus reduce the burden both of us have laid on larger groups and their continuities.

Indeed, were I to rewrite now I should put a little more individualism into the history. This cryptic expression means that I would try to make the process of canon building and interpretation more historical and more personal at the same time. History should be viewed as the work of individuals and groups, not just of sociological or theological forces. Morton Smith's ideas about Palestinian parties as shapers of the Old Testament may be slightly exaggerated, but nobody can deny that some persons in some group wanted the biblical books that were chosen and rejected the ones that were not. Neither canonization nor exegesis has ever been the work of impersonal forces. Even the idea of "the modern" is something loved and espoused by some, neglected by others, rejected by not a few. Is modernity itself somehow canonical? For a discussion we turn to Tracy's conclusion.

R. M. G.

16

Interpretation of the Bible and Interpretation Theory

As the history of biblical interpretation in preceding chapters demonstrates, the rise of historical consciousness in the nineteenth and twentieth centuries has proved the major innovation in biblical interpretation since the earlier rise of an allegorical method. So central has historical critical interpretation of the Bible become for all theology that it is inconceivable that any contemporary Christian theologian (except for a strict fundamentalist) would not feel obliged to pay attention to the results of historico-critical exegesis. Yet, as the last chapter argued, to pay attention to those results is not the equivalent of becoming captive to historico-critical conclusions. The age-old question, therefore, reemerges: what is a properly theological interpretation of the Bible in a historically conscious age?

This question has been intensified in the last fifteen years for many biblical scholars and theologians by the rise of an explicit concern with hermeneutics or interpretation theory across the disciplines. In one sense, this concern is already represented in every chapter of this volume by the analyses of the different, often conflicting, methods and theories of interpretation in Christian history. Indeed, the contemporary turn to hermeneutics in biblical studies can be viewed as an explicit theoretical reflection on the history of interpretation recounted in the earlier chapters. It is impossible to understand contemporary biblical hermeneutics without recalling the history of biblical interpretation. It is also impossible that the contemporary concern with hermeneutics could have occurred without the emergence of historical consciousness in Western culture and the use of the historico-critical methodology by biblical exegetes.

Nevertheless, each of the particular forms of contemporary interest in hermeneutics demands explicit treatment. Debates on the nature of hermeneutics continue to flourish. Biblical scholars propose candidate after candidate (structuralism, semiotics, deconstruction, among others). It seems imperative, therefore, first to sort out what hermeneutics is and what difference it makes for contemporary theology and biblical studies. This chapter will address the first task by describing the main claims of hermeneutics. The last two chapters will address the difference hermeneutics thus conceived makes for biblical studies and theology.

INTERPRETATION THEORY

The problem of interpretation becomes a central issue in cultural periods of crisis. So it was for the Stoics and their reinterpretation of the Greek and Roman myths. So it was for those Jews and Christians who developed the allegorical method. And so it is for Jews and Christians since the emergence of historical consciousness. The sense of distance that many contemporary Westerners feel in relationship to the classics of the culture (including the scriptures) impels an explicit interest in the process of interpretation itself. But if scholars focus only on their sense of historical distance from the classics, they can be tempted to formulate the problem of interpretation as primarily that of *avoiding misunderstanding*. Even Schleiermacher, justly credited as the founder of modern hermeneutics, often tended to formulate the problem of hermeneutics in this manner. One aspect of Schleiermacher's hermeneutics (his famous emphasis on 'empathy' and 'divination') tended to encourage the development of a Romantic hermeneutics. The other aspect of Schleiermacher's hermeneutics (his emphasis on developing methodical controls to avoid misunderstanding) tended to encourage the development of strictly methodological interests—first historico-critical, then formalist.

The fruits of the impasse occasioned by those two conflicting tendencies remain central in the present debate. For many theories of interpretation, the principal insight is into the actuality of historical, cultural, and often religious distance (and hence a sense of 'alienation') from the classics, including the scriptures. The central problem is the need to avoid misunderstanding. The central hope is in the controls afforded by some method, principally the historico-critical method. There is no doubt that historico-critical methods are needed to keep interpreters from forcing these texts of alien cultures or earlier periods of one's own culture into the horizon of present self-understanding. The rise of historico-critical methods in modern scripture studies has provided the best assurance that exegesis remain ex-egesis and not an undisciplined eis-egesis.

Most contemporary interpreters of the Bible not only accept but demand the controls and the clear gains that historical methods have allowed. Without those methods, the alternatives seem bleak: either an ahistorical reading of the Bible in an age marked above all by historical consciousness; or a fundamentalist, ever more brittle insistence that modernity's commitment to historical consciousness has been a fatal error.

It is impossible in so short a space to exhaust the complex debates on hermeneutics in the modern period. It is clear, however, that the contribution of Hans-Georg Gadamer has been fundamental both for general interpretation theory and for the interpretation of the Bible. Gadamer's major significance is that he developed an interpretation theory that was historically conscious without being strictly historicist. Moreover, he could maintain this position without retreating into Romantic pleas for empathy with "the mind and/or spirit" of the author. The major interest of the present work is not in the Heideggerian ontology (or 'historicity') of Gadamer's position. It is rather in his claims for the actual process of interpreting texts. This process is present in the interpretation of such classic religious texts as the Bible. The process itself can be described in the following terms.

In the first place every interpreter enters the task of interpretation with some preunderstanding of the subject matter addressed by the text. Contemporary historical consciousness helps to clarify the complex reality of the interpreter's preunderstanding. Historical consciousness is after all a post-Enlightenment, and in some ways even an anti-Enlightenment, phenomenon. More exactly, the Enlightenment belief that the interpreter can in principle and should in fact eliminate all "prejudgments" was at best a half-truth. The truth operative in the Enlightenment's "prejudice against prejudgments" (Gadamer) was classically expressed by Kant as *"aude*

sapere" (dare to think for yourself [and free yourself from the mys-
tifications and obscurantisms present in all the traditions]). Indeed,
that critical force released by the Enlightenment was a liberating
moment that inevitably forms part of the horizon (the preunderstanding) of any modern scholar, including the biblical scholar.

Yet the reason why this Enlightenment truth is only a half-truth
must also be clarified. If historicity is not merely a philosophical
abstraction and the terms *socialization* or *enculturation* are other
than disciplinary jargon, they all bespeak the other truth, missed
by Enlightenment and by modern methodological polemics against
'prejudgments' and 'traditions'. The fact is that no interpreter enters into the attempt to understand any text or any historical event
without prejudgments formed by the history of the effects of her or
his culture. There does not exist any exegete or historian as purely
autonomous as the Enlightenment model promised. This recognition of the inevitable presence of tradition in all preunderstanding,
moreover, does not require that the interpreter share the tradition
to which the text to be interpreted belongs. The claim does not
mean, for example, that interpreters of the Bible need believe in a
particular tradition in order to interpret it properly. It does mean,
however, that every interpreter enters into the act of interpretation
bearing the history of the effects, conscious and unconscious, of
the traditions to which all ineluctably belong. For each of us belongs to history far more than history belongs to us. Any claim
that the interpreter can ignore the history of those effects is finally
self-deceptive.

Consider, for example, what happens in the use of any language. Every language carries with it the history of the effects, the
traditions, of that language. The word *religion*, for example, as
used in the English language, carries with it history of the effects
of both the Roman notions of "civil religion," Jewish and Christian
notions of 'faith', and Enlightenment notions of 'natural' and 'positive' religion. No one who speaks or writes English escapes that
tradition. No one who thinks in and through a particular language
(and who does not?) escapes the history of the effects—the traditions—inevitably present in that language. We can note, therefore,
a first matter of fact for every interpreter: no interpreter enters the
process of interpretation without some prejudgments: included in

those prejudgments through the very language we speak and write is the history of the effects of the traditions forming that language.

Yet the fact that we say that the interpreter "enters" the process of interpretation also allows us to recognize a second step in that process. That second step includes a second matter of fact. The clearest way to see this second step is to consider our actual experience of any classic text, image, symbol, event, ritual, or person. Indeed, any classic text (such as a text of the Bible) can be considered paradigmatic for the interpretation of all texts. First, it is an inevitable aspect of life in any culture that classics exist. Those classics, both consciously and unconsciously, deeply influence the history of the effects of the preunderstanding of all participants in that culture. For example, every Westerner is initially startled when attempting to interpret the seeming dissolution of the self in classic Buddhist texts. The belief in individuality among Westerners is not limited to substance notions of the self. Even radical critiques of the notion of the 'self as substance' in the West live by means of the history of the effects of Jewish and Christian senses of the responsible self in the presence of the radically monotheistic God; the Greek and Roman senses of the ethical, political, the contemplative, and active self; and all the other reformulations of the importance of a self from Burckhardt's Renaissance individual through Kierkegaard's or Nietzsche's radical individual to modern suspicions of traditional understandings of the self-as-individual. The history of the effects of the Jewish, Greek, Roman, Medieval, Renaissance, Reformation, and modern senses of the reality and importance of a 'self' mean that some such effect is likely to be present in the preunderstanding of any Western thinker.

When attempting to interpret a classic Buddhist text, therefore, we are startled not only by the questions and responses on the meaning of self in these texts. We are startled as well into a recognition of how deeply any language, any tradition, and, therefore, any preunderstanding is affected by this Western insistence on the importance of an individual self.

When interpreting any *classic* text in our own Western traditions, moreover, we may note that these texts bear a certain permanence and excess of meaning that resists a "definitive" interpretation. Thus are we faced with the first productive paradox of the classic. The actual experience of any classic text in the Bible vexes, provokes, elicits a claim to serious attention which we cannot evade. We are, as Karl Barth insisted, tempted to enter into the "strange, new world" of the Bible. And just this claim to attention from the classic text provokes the reader's preunderstanding into a dual recognition, first, of how formed our preunderstanding is and, at the same time, a sense of the 'vexing' or 'provocation' elicited by the claim to attention of this text. In sum the interpreter finds her- or himself now forced into the activity of interpreting in order to understand. An interpreter's first recognition is the claim to attention provoked by the text. The experience may range from a tentative sense of resonance with the question posed by the text through senses of import or even shock.

At this point, the interpreter may search for some heuristic model to understand the complex process of interaction now set in motion by the claim to attention of the text and its disclosure of one's preunderstanding. This search for a heuristic model for the de facto process of interpretation provides the third step of interpretation. Gadamer's now famous and controversial suggestion of the model of the "game of conversation" for this process of interpretation is relevant here. Gadamer's insight is that the model of conversation is not imposed upon our actual experience of interpretation as some new *de jure* method, norm, or rule. Rather the phenomenon of the conversation aptly describes the de facto experience of interpreting any classic text. To understand how this occurs, first consider the more general phenomenon of the game before describing the game of conversation itself.

The key to any game is not the self-consciousness of the players in the game but rather the release of self-consciousness into a consciousness of the phenomenon of the to-and-fro, the back-and-forth movements which constitute the game itself. The attitudes of authentic players of any game depend above all upon this nature of the game itself. If the game is allowed to take over, then the back-and-forth movements take over the players. In any game, it is not our opponents so much as it is the game that plays us. If we cannot release ourselves to that back-and-forth movement, we cannot play. But if we can play, we experience ourselves as caught up in the movement of the game. We realize that our usual self-con-

sciousness cannot be the key here. Rather, we may even find however temporarily a sense of a new self in, by, and through the actual playing, the release to the to-and-fro movements of the game.

This common human experience of the game is the key to the
basic model of conversation for the "game" of interpretation. For
what is authentic conversation (as distinct from debate, gossip, or
confrontation) other than the ability to become caught up in the to-
and-fro movement of the logic of question and response? Just as
the subjects in any game release themselves from self-consciousness in order to play, so too in every authentic conversation the
subject is released by the to-and-fro movement of the subject matter under discussion. It is true, of course, that conversation is ordinarily a phenomenon between two living subjects or even one subject reflecting on a question.

Yet the model of conversation, as Gadamer correctly insists, is
also in fact applicable to our experience of the interpretation of
texts. For if interpreters allow the claim of the text to serious attention to provoke their questioning, then they enter into the logic of
question and response. And that logic is nothing other than the
particular form which the to-and-fro movement of this singular
game, the conversation, takes. The kind of interaction which occurs when we converse is, in fact, the interaction whereby the subject matter, not our own subjectivity, is allowed to take over. If we
cannot converse, if we cannot allow for the demands of any subject matter—any questions provoked by the claim to attention of
the text—then we cannot interpret. But if we have even once entered into any genuine conversation, then we are willing to admit
that conversation can be a model for the process of interpretation
itself.

Along with the demands of historico-critical method, therefore,
interpreters need to allow a conversation with the formed subject
matter—the questions and responses of the text even with the
"strange, new world" of the biblical texts. On the hermeneutical
model, therefore, the primary meaning of the text does not lie "behind" it (in the mind of the author, in the original social setting, in
the original audience) nor even "in" the text itself. Rather, the
meaning of the text lies *in front of* the text—in the now *common*
question, the now common subject matter of both text and inter-

preter. Historically conscious interpreters do not seek simply to repeat, to reproduce the original meaning of the text, in order to understand its (and now their) questions. Rather, they employ all the
tools of historical criticism and then seek to mediate, translate, interpret the meaning into their present horizon. Interpreters seek, in
Gadamer's often misunderstood phrase, to "fuse the horizon" of
the text (the horizon of meaning in front of the text) with our own
horizon.

By recognizing the actual experience of the interaction of interpreter and text as an experience of conversation, moreover, Gadamer maintains that interpreters may also recognize the inevitable
finitude and historicity of even their best acts of interpretation. For
they may recognize the fate of all interpretation of classics as a
fate that can become, when embraced as a conversation, a destiny.
That destiny—present in all the classic conversations, especially
the Platonic dialogues, and common to all the great interpreters of
the Bible—is the insight that "Insofar as we understand at all we
understand differently [from the original author]."

Hermeneutics, therefore, insists that the historico-critical
method is essential for any historically conscious interpretation.
Hermeneutics equally insists that interpreters have not finished
their task with the use of that method. As we shall see in the next
two chapters, biblical interpreters complete their historico-critical
work only to begin the second phase of their hermeneutical task: a
conversation with the subject matter—the questions and responses—of the biblical text. As we already saw in earlier chapters, this process began for Christian theology as early as the interpretations of the Jewish scriptures by Jesus and Paul.

AFTER GADAMER: HERMENEUTICS OF SUSPICION
AND EXPLANATORY METHODS

From the many discussions of Gadamer's interpretation theory,
two crucial questions have been posed. Both have direct relevance
for biblical studies. The first question is whether Gadamer's theory
involves too sanguine a notion of tradition. One need not retreat to
Enlightenment polemics against the inevitable presence of tradition
in all understanding in order to share the insistence of several of

Gadamer's critics (especially Jürgen Habermas) that Gadamer's notion of tradition bears its own danger.

One way of clarifying that danger is to recall the truth about the Enlightenment itself: namely, it believed in the emancipatory thrust of critical reason. Yet this is not a charge against Gadamer's own general program of interpretation, only against his particular interpretation of the Enlightenment. For whatever the truth of Gadamer's interpretation of the Enlightenment (for me, it is the partial truth of the corrective of naïve Enlightenment polemics against tradition), his general position on interpretation does not stand or fall on the truth of that particular interpretation. As much as his critics, like Habermas, Gadamer too allows for, indeed demands, moments of critical reflection intrinsic to the process of interpretation. The fact that his position is grounded in the conversation between text *and* interpreter (not simply in the text, as in purely formalist criticism) indicates this. It is true that the critical reflection which Gadamer characteristically endorses is akin to the classic reflection expressed in the dialogues of Plato and the phenomenology of Aristotle rather than that in modern critical theories.

However, even those differences should not allow critics to assume that Gadamer is simply a traditionalist unconcerned with critical analysis of the tradition. The real difficulty lies elsewhere. Gadamer's retrieval of tradition's enrichment of the interpreter's preunderstanding does include forms of critical reflection that can undo error and falsity in any interpretation. Yet it remains an open question whether Gadamer's understanding of the kind of critical reflection available to the modern interpreter can really account for those modern critical theories developed to expose not error, but illusion; not normal, cognitive, and moral ambiguity, but systematic distortions. Here is where Gadamer's anti-Enlightenment polemic severely damages his case. His apprehension is that any move to critical theory will inevitably become yet another futile attempt to provide a mythical 'presuppositionless' interpreter. Because of that apprehension Gadamer seems to discount the occasional necessity of some critical theory in some conversations— including conversations with such classics as the Bible. The basic developments in modern hermeneutics (as in liberal and modernist theological interpretations of the Bible) have been geared to various critical theories that were forged to expose the latent meanings of texts—especially those latent meanings that enforce not mere error but illusion, not occasional difficulties but systematic distortions.

But Gadamer's own position does not really allow these so-called 'hermeneutics of suspicion' to join his 'hermeneutics of retrieval or recovery'. Yet our common human experience of interpretation as conversation should alert us to this occasional need for a hermeneutics of suspicion and its attendant critical theory. To return to the example of interpersonal conversation for a moment: If, in the course of a conversation, we begin to suspect (the verb is apt) that our conversation partner is psychotic, we would be justified in suspending the conversation. In a post-Freudian culture the need for suspicion and the need for critical theories (such as psychoanalytic theory) to spot and heal systematic distortions in our personal, cultural, and social lives has become an indispensable aspect of any modern interpreter's preunderstanding. It is true, of course, that such interpretation of latent, hidden, or repressed meanings unconsciously operative as systematic distortions is easier to develop (thanks to psychoanalysis) on the personal and interpersonal levels than it is on the social, cultural, and historical levels. However, even on those levels various forms of Marxist 'ideology critique' and (more recently, with thinkers such as Foucault) various forms of Nietzschean 'genealogical methods' exist to try to locate the systematic distortions in both the preunderstanding of the interpreter and in the classic texts and traditions of the culture. Every one of these hermeneutics of suspicion, moreover, cannot rest simply on the model of conversation. Each needs a critical theory to aid its operation.

For an interpreter who suspects that there *may* be systematic distortions in a tradition, a hermeneutics of suspicion can be a helpful correlate to a hermeneutics of recovery. At such points of recognition of systematic distortion, the hermeneutic model of conversation becomes inadequate to describe the full process of interpretation. Recall the model of psychoanalysis on the interpersonal level of interpretation, for example. The analyst and the analysand are not, in fact, engaged in a conversation *tout simple*. Rather, they are engaged in a process of interpretation whereby one conversation partner (the analyst) employs a critical theory (psychoanalytic theory) to aid the other partner in interpreting her or his experience. Thereby the interpretation may emancipate the second partner from the systematic distortions that are repressed but operative in experience. Only after such emancipation is the hermeneutic conversation which Gadamer insists upon for all interpretation possible again. Yet not to face that demand for suspicion in interpreting both ourselves and our traditions (including religious traditions) seems to leave us, unwittingly, without the full hermeneutic resources which our era renders available. Just as Gadamer's hermeneutics of recovery as conversation can complement exegesis of a strict historico-critical sort, so too any legitimate hermeneutics of suspicion can complement the hermeneutics of recovery.

Conversation remains the key heuristic model for hermeneutics. And yet, as the earlier chapters discussing the liberals and modernists suggested and as later chapters on contemporary postliberal theological interpretations of scripture will suggest, the model of conversation alone is necessary but not sufficient for the needs and aims of contemporary interpretation of the Bible. It is important to insist, moreover, that this correction of Gadamer's position need not demand a retreat to an Enlightenment polemic against all tradition. But it does demand the development of modern critical theories whose emancipatory thrust continues the kind of critical reflection present in the logic of questioning in the Platonic dialogues, in the legitimate demands of historico-critical methods, and in the model of interpretation as conversation set forth by Gadamer himself.

This first difficulty with Gadamer's position has occasioned, therefore, a basic acceptance of his model for interpretation as conversation while also requiring a corrective for his critique of the role of 'critical theory' in the interpretative process as a whole. The second question posed by post-Gadamer hermeneutics (including biblical hermeneutics) is related not to the model of conversation but to the notion of the text and its subject matter. The crucial issue is this: The subject matter which becomes common to both interpreter and text in the process of interpretation as conversation is one whose claim to attention is *expressed in the form of a text.*

This point is worth emphasizing in order to understand the contemporary debates on hermeneutics.

Once again (as with the need for a hermeneutics of suspicion and critical theory) it is not that Gadamer is unaware of the importance of form and structure for *expressing* the subject matter and thereby, on his terms, for causing the claim to serious attention of the meaning in front of the text.

But insofar as the interpreter recognizes that the text produces its claim to attention by structuring and forming the subject matter into a work, an ordered whole, *a text,* we must also recognize the legitimacy of using some explanatory methods in the interpretation. It is true, as Paul Ricoeur insists along with Gadamer, that *Verstehen* (understanding) envelops the entire process of interpretation. But it is also true, as Ricoeur correctly insists against Gadamer, that *Erklären* (explanatory methods) can develop our understanding of how the meaning is produced through the very form and structure of the text.

A fuller model of conversation thereby suggests itself: namely, that the entire process of interpretation encompasses some initial understanding yielding to an explanation of the way the referent (the world of meaning in front of the text) is produced through the meanings-in-form-and-structures in the texts. After those explanatory moments the reader has, in fact, a better understanding of the subject matter (as *in-formed* subject matter) than any interpreter does without them. Indeed, without the use of such explanatory methods as formalist literary criticism or even semiotic and structuralist methods, it is difficult to see how, against Gadamer's own manifest intentions, the interpreter is not in danger of simply extracting messages (under the rubric 'subject matter') from the complex, structured, formed subject matter which is the text.

Every text, after all, is a structural whole. Every subject matter comes to us with a claim to serious attention in and through its form and structure. To resist explanatory methods seems pointless. For such methods can show how expression occurs from the semiotic level of the word, through the semantics of the sentence and the structured whole of the text (achieved principally through composition and genre), to the individuating power of style. So apprehensive can hermeneutical thinkers become on how *Erklären* (explanation) can serve as a means to undo conversation between text and interpreter (and, therefore, undo authentic hermeneutical *Verstehen* [understanding]) that they are sometimes tempted to discount explanatory methods altogether.

The temptation to methodologism is real enough. But, *pace* Oscar Wilde, it is not true that the only way to resist temptation is to yield to it. Rather, interpreters should use any explanatory method that shows how meaning is produced in the text (e.g., genre analysis in biblical studies). Structuralist methods, for example, are not identical with the ideologies of some structuralist thinkers any more than Gadamer's own hermeneutics is identical with his commitments to the Greek and German humanist traditions or his polemics against the Enlightenment and modern critical theories. Rather, structuralist methods—the formalist methods of the New Critics, the *explication du texte* methods of earlier Continental critics, semiotic methods, the more familiar use of literary criticism by historical critics, or even some variants of deconstructionist methods—have demonstrated their hermeneutical value even to those interpreters who do not share the larger and often monist claims of some proponents. In the following chapters we shall see how these methods are presently used by biblical scholars.

Explanatory methods in fact develop or challenge, even confront, one's initial understanding of how the subject matter comes to be expressed in and through its structure and form. In Ricoeur's technical formulation, this may be restated as the ability of these explanatory methods to show how the "sense" of the work produces the "referent" of the work. Understanding and explanation (like truth *and* method, historico-critical methods and hermeneutics) need not be implacable enemies. They can become, for any interpreter, allies—albeit wary and uneasy allies. The wider conversation of the contemporary conflict on interpretation theory need not yield to the spectacle of armed camps. Rather, real possibilities exist for the whole community of interpreters in all disciplines to engage in authentic conversation.

And nowhere are those possibilities more alive with all the "blooming, buzzing confusion" of experience than in the interpretation of that most puzzling, pluralistic, and genuinely ambiguous of all phenomena, religion. Why religious texts such as the Bible have become a paradigmatic text case for all theories of interpretation will be the concern of the remaining chapters. In Western culture as a whole, biblical interpretation is often the principal locus where every major new theory of interpretation is best tested. We have seen several examples of that process of testing in the earlier chapters. This present chapter has been concerned to clarify the major options in the contemporary debates on interpretation theory. It is time, however, to see how those debates function in the pluralistic world of contemporary interpretations of the Bible.

17

Theological Interpretation
of the Bible Today

THEOLOGY AS INTERPRETATION OF THE BIBLE:
GENERAL RUBRICS

The fact that interpretation has become a central issue has inevitably influenced the interpretation of the Bible. As contemporary literary critics have joined their historical critical colleagues in biblical interpretation, provocative new interpretations of the Bible have appeared. Both the Hebrew scripture (e.g., Robert Alter) and the New Testament (e.g., Frank Kermode) are being interpreted by means of new literary-critical methods—semiotics, structuralism, deconstruction. Other literary critics (e.g., Northrup Frye) have expanded their concern to reinterpreting the role of the Bible (as the "great code" pervading Western culture itself).

The principal aim of this work, however, is not to analyze the new interpretations of the 'Bible as literature' and the 'Bible in literature and culture'. Rather the aim is to understand how theological interpretations of the Bible have been influenced by the concern with interpretation summarized in the preceding chapter. Indeed, it is the turn to interpretation theory across disciplines that has rendered the once-firm division between theological and secular interpretations of the Bible more flexible than in the past.

On the model of interpretation as a conversation with the questions in the text, it is no longer possible to divide the task so easily as it once seemed. It is true, of course, that biblical texts can also be literature. As such, they remain fully open to literary critical analysis of the various new schools. Yet these same literary texts are also religious texts raising and responding to—often through provocative new uses of literary genres—explicitly religious questions. Critics such as Paul Ricoeur have suggested that explicitly religious uses of any genre characteristically intensify, radicalize, and often transgress more familiar uses. So it becomes more difficult for literary critics to ignore the religious questions of the scriptural texts.

For genre is now widely recognized as being not merely a way of classifying meanings already present but productive of new meaning as well. Therefore the meanings produced through explicitly religious uses of a genre (e.g., proverb, parable, or narrative) include religious questions which can no longer be neatly bracketed out of consideration by an interpreter of the scriptural texts.

Some traditional alternatives for biblical interpretation, therefore, seem spent. For characteristically there were two—and only two—options for biblical interpretation. The first was a purely secular interpretation that set aside the religious concerns of the text to study its literary qualities; the second, a purely theological interpretation that demanded faith in the revelation to which the texts attest. This traditional distinction can no longer function as neatly as it once did.

It is true that both these alternatives still can and do function. There will continue to be theological interpretations of the scriptures for and within the believing church community. There are and should be historio-critical interpretations of these texts using every possible method (including the new literary critical methods) to articulate strictly and solely historical conclusions. Yet once the concern with interpretation theory becomes central in any discipline it becomes clear that this familiar division of alternatives is not exhaustive. For, as discussed in chapter 16, interpretation is fundamentally a conversation with the subject-matter (the questions and responses of any text). That subject matter is itself expressed and thereby produced by such strategies as grammar, semiotics, semantics, genre, and style. Hence, the interpreter of the subject matter of religious text must risk a conversation with the religious questions expressed in and through the text itself.

Historians can ignore these religious questions whenever they approach the text as an occasion for historical knowledge of the event or events expressed or implied by the text itself. But interpreters of the text's subject matter cannot imitate the historians' approach. For if we are interpreting the text for its own sake, and not the text as a clue to some other reality—for example, the occurrence or nonoccurrence of historical events—the historio-critical model is not a sufficient method of interpretation.

For biblical texts express both literary and religious concerns. To interpret them we must be willing, precisely as interpreters of *these* texts, to risk a conversation with their questions and concerns. The model of interpretation as conversation has encouraged a subtle shift in secular interpretations of the Bible from The Bible as literature to the "Bible as religious literature." The study of the explicitly religious use of any genre has coaxed many modern literary critics informed by the contemporary debate in interpretation theory into wary, but real, engagement with the religious questions of the scriptural texts—questions expressed in and through the literary forms themselves.

The same blurring of familiar boundaries has occurred in theological interpretations of the Bible as well. Once again, the use of the model of conversation has encouraged this change. An earlier theological model could assume that theological interpretation of the Bible required the theologian to be a believer in the revelation witnessed to in the scriptural texts. In fact, of course, most theologians are believers. But the matter of hermeneutical principle is far more complex.

For if the interpretation of text involves conversation with the questions and responses of the text, this means, for theology too, genuine *conversation*. The single option of traditional theological self-understanding (namely, the theologian interpreter of the Bible must have faith in the Bible) was, at best, too simple a formulation. The hermeneutical model of conversation suggests that theology must reconsider a fuller spectrum of genuinely theological interpretations of the Bible. This means that sometimes the theologian will approach a full conversation with the biblical text with the response of faith. At other times the theologian may approach the text with the religious question of the text firmly in view but without necessarily sharing the faith of the Christian community. What each of these options along the fuller spectrum of theological interpretations of the Bible means we can only see clearly, however, after examining the nature of theological interpretation itself.

Theology, in both its traditional and its contemporary forms, is interpretation. More exactly, theology is an interpretation of a religious tradition for the sake of the religious tradition itself. As earlier chapters have shown, modes of theological interpretation have shifted, often radically, over the centuries. But that theology is an interpretive discipline from beginning to end has remained constant.

When interpretation becomes a major issue for all disciplines, this too affects theology. Today, therefore, theology becomes not merely interpretation but self-conscious interpretation. This singular cultural fact provides for a new but not radically different understanding of theology's task. Let us start with a widely accepted definition of that theological task in the contemporary period. Christian theology is the attempt to establish mutually critical correlations between an interpretation of the Christian tradition and an interpretation of the contemporary situation. This so-called "revised correlation method" for theology is in fact nothing other than a hermeneutically self-conscious clarification and correction of traditional theology.

Let us consider each element in the definition to see why this is so. To attempt to establish 'mutually critical correlations' between two sets of interpretations is an expansive way to acknowledge that theology is an interpretation of the tradition in an ever-changing cultural situation. The phrase 'mutually critical correlations' also explicates what otherwise remains merely implicit: the fact that there is no general model which can be allowed to determine any particular interpretation. Rather, there is a general heuristic model of correlation that can guide but not determine each particular interpretation. Such a heuristic model is helpful insofar as it alerts theologians that they always interpret the Christian tradition for concrete situations. There is no nonsituational basis for any interpretation.

As interpreters theologians are attempting to correlate their situational preunderstanding to the same particular classic texts of the tradition. By using the heuristic model of correlation to guide that interpretation, theologians are simply reminding themselves that their task is interpretation as conversation with the subject matter of the text. As in genuine conversation, one cannot determine the

outcome before the actual interpretation. One can, however, recognize that every theological interpretation will correlate in some
manner the claim to attention of the text and the preunderstanding
of the situation.

In the course of interpretation as conversation, this correlation
may suggest that in a particular case there is a radical confrontation between text and situation. The confrontation occurs, for example, if the creation narratives in Genesis are read as scientific
rather than religious texts. In another instance the correlation may
reveal genuine analogies or similarities-in-difference between the
meaning expressed in the text and contemporary situational self-
understanding. This possibility occurs, for example, in Bultmann's
correlation of the anthropology in Paul and John with contemporary existentialist understandings of 'authentic existence'. In still
other cases, the correlation may suggest an identity of meaning between text and situation. This possibility occurs, for example, in
liberation theology's correlation of the struggles of the tribes of
Israel in the Exodus accounts with contemporary movements for
political liberation.

The important point, however, is not any of these concrete examples of familiar contemporary interpretation. Each example is in
fact a deliberately controversial one that may or may not ring true
to the reader; any example of any concrete biblical interpretation
will do. The major point is that interpretation as a conversation between text and interpreter on the religious subject matter can be
described, in properly general terms, as a correlation. For a correlation logically allows a full spectrum of possible interpretations
ranging from a confrontation (first example) through a similarity-
in-difference (second example) to an identity (third example).

The model of correlation is, therefore, simply a general heuristic
guide to alert theological interpreters that they must attend to three
realities: first, the inevitable presence of the interpreter's own preunderstanding (situation); second, the claim to attention of the text
itself; third, the conversation as some form of correlation (identity,
similarity, or confrontation).

The other elements in the definition of theology in fact merely
render more explicit this intrinsically hermeneutical understanding
of theology itself. To call the correlation one that establishes 'mu-

tually critical correlations' is to state that neither text nor interpreter, but only the conversation between both can rule. Interpreters cannot abandon their preunderstanding, nor can the claims of
texts to the attention of that preunderstanding be abandoned. Text
and interpreter must be allowed to be mutually critical. Each must
enter into a genuine conversation with the subject matter of the
text itself—now become the common subject matter of text and
interpreter.

The revised model of correlation used by many contemporary
theologians is fundamentally a hermeneutical model. The demanding process of interpretation as conversation must be allowed full
scope. Any particular correlation may occur in a more complex
fashion than the description thus far may suggest. More precisely,
theologians are likely to engage in two distinct moves in the single
process of interpretation. This means that they often enter into the
interpretation of the Bible with an explicit, not merely implicit
preunderstanding. Much theological labor is spent indeed in interpreting the cultural situation in order to clarify the religious questions theologians might ask of the biblical text.

Again, this familiar move does not change the basic hermeneutical situation. It merely makes explicit by rendering self-con-
sciously hermeneutical the fuller meaning of the theologian's
preunderstanding. No preunderstanding can ever be rendered fully
self-conscious, of course. No one is ever fully conscious of all the
effects of traditions and personal life-history upon one's self-understanding. But what we can do—and what contemporary theologians do attempt under the rubric of interpretation of our cultural
situation—is to render that preunderstanding as explicit as possible. They do so by interpreting the principal religious questions in
the contemporary situation. For some theologians the principal
question may be about mortality; for others, guilt and responsibil-
ity, radical anxiety or fundamental trust, joy or peace in daily life;
for still others, radical alienation or oppression. In every case theologians by interpreting the principal religious question(s) in the
contemporary situation are making explicit one major facet of their
own preunderstanding. Thus can the conversation as a correlation
with the biblical text proceed with greater exactitude.

Many theologians of correlation speak of correlating two sets of interpretations: the interpretation of the present situation and the interpretation of the tradition. This is accurate enough so long as it means that the religious questions in the situation are rendered as explicit as possible before the interpretation of the biblical text begins. Indeed this is a positive development insofar as it clarifies to some extent the concrete nature of the preunderstanding with which the theologian enters the process of interpreting the biblical text. Yet once that concrete interpretation begins, all earlier situational analyses are also put at risk by the conversation itself. It is not only our present answers but also our questions which are risked when we enter a conversation with a classic text. For all prior interpretations of our own preunderstanding, like all our prior interpretations of the text, are at risk whenever we enter a genuine conversation. This conversation will be the necessary interaction between our preunderstanding and the text insofar as both are governed by the questions and responses of the now *common* subject matter in the to-and-fro movements of the conversation. "Insofar as we understand at all we understand differently!"

The same kind of risk, we must note anew, occurs on the side of all our previous theological interpretations of the biblical text itself. Indeed, the most dangerous move for a Christian fundamentalist is to enter into the risk of a genuine conversation with the biblical text. There one may well find (in fundamentalist interpretations of Genesis one clearly will find) that the text itself challenges prior fundamentalist preunderstandings. If interpretation *is* genuine conversation then all prior interpretation of both our preunderstanding and the text are now put at risk. There is no way, prior to the conversation itself, to determine the "correct" theological interpretation of the biblical texts.

Theologians, therefore, are in no different hermeneutical position than other interpreters. By rendering that hermeneutical position explicit by means of the revised theological method of correlation they clarify their own situation as hermeneutical. In this general model theologians too find a spectrum of possible responses ranging from confrontation through similarity to identity. These general principles of theological interpretation on the model of correlation remain general heuristic models to guide interpretation, never to determine it. As general principles, the model of correlation seems both clarifying and serviceable for the whole range of nonfundamentalist theological interpretations of the Bible. For more particular rubrics for theological interpretation, however, we must turn to equally important questions concerning the nature of the biblical texts being interpreted and the role of the Christian community in theological interpretation.

THEOLOGY AND THE INTERPRETATION OF THE BIBLE: TEXT AND EVENT

Thus far we have endeavored to clarify two central issues for the theological interpretation of the Bible: The preceding chapter focussed on the contemporary question of hermeneutical theory; the first section of this chapter concentrated on the relevance of hermeneutical theory for the correlation model of theological interpretation. Now begins the central topic: the theological interpretation of scripture. But one further set of issues requires clarification for understanding the fuller dimensions of that task: namely, the role and nature of the biblical texts in theological self-understanding.

In one sense earlier chapters have already broached these issues. In another sense, however, we must see how these issues are formulated in the contemporary context of theological interpretation. In the preceding section the nature of an interpretation of the situation (and thereby the preunderstanding of the theologian in a theological hermeneutics) was discussed at some length. At the same time the interpretation of the Christian tradition and the role of the scriptures in that tradition was then consigned to a relatively general and fluid statement. It is time, however, to correct that generality by specifying the issues demanding attention before the fuller discussion of the role of the Bible in theological interpretation can be clarified.

The first issue is that of the relationship of text and event in biblical texts. From the Christian perspective, the biblical texts play a real but limited normative role. For the Christian community its own decision to establish a canon of the Bible expressed not only a historical but also a crucial theological decision. The historical facts of canon formation are difficult to unravel. Yet the theological import of that historical series of decisions by the Christian communities can scarcely be exaggerated. For to establish a canon means that the community no longer has only a series of honored religious texts (analogous to the role of the classic Vedic hymns in Hinduism). The Christian community now has a series of canonical texts that have become sacred scriptures. The central Christian affirmation has been and remains, I believe *in* Jesus Christ *with* the apostles.

The fundamental Christian belief is a belief *in* the revelatory event of Jesus Christ present in the community now. Yet this belief, it is important to recall, is a belief *in* Jesus Christ that is also qualified by the phrase "with the apostles." The epoch-making establishment of a canon meant, therefore, that the Christian community affirmed that its present and future belief in Jesus Christ is a belief that must always prove in continuity "with the apostles." So the principal issue is not the nature of the theological criteria of 'apostolicity' or other criteria the Christian communities may have used in establishing the canon. The principal theological import of the canon is that the writings known as the 'apostolic writings' became the scriptural New Testament. The canonical fact of the New Testament, moreover, became the occasion for the Christian community—guided by its belief *in* Jesus Christ *with* the apostles—to appropriate the Hebrew scriptures as the Christian Old Testament.

The Christian church now possessed a collection of texts which could be called in the strict sense scripture. It now became *theologically* crucial to judge every later theological statement in terms of its appropriateness to the apostolic witness expressed normatively in the scriptures.

Theological hermeneutics of these religious texts now understood as scriptures therefore remains committed to developing theological understanding of Christian witness in and for every new, concrete situation. Yet these ever new interpretations should be worked out in a manner which, negatively, does not contradict and, positively, is appropriate to the original apostolic witness in the scriptures. Just as there remains a constant theological need to develop criteria of intelligibility for the Christian witness to every concrete situation, there remains an equally constant need to develop criteria of appropriateness for every contemporary Christian witness to the original apostolic witness in the scriptures.

To call these latter criteria of appropriateness is to choose a deliberately flexible word. For *appropriateness* does not suggest that a later Christian witness must be found in identical form in the scriptures. Nor does appropriateness suggest that there can be no criticism of scriptural expressions in the light of later developments. Criteria of appropriateness insist that all later theologies in *Christian* theology are obliged to show why they are not in radical disharmony with the central Christian witness expressed in the scriptures. In that restricted sense, scripture, as the original apostolic witness to Jesus Christ, norms but is not normed (*norma normans sed not normata*) by later witnesses.

The central role of the scriptures within Christian self-understanding forces, therefore, careful consideration of the nature of the biblical texts themselves. The first question to note is that the scriptures play a central role in Christian self-understanding, yet, in terms of the scriptural witness, Christianity cannot be considered strictly a religion of the book. Like Judaism but unlike Islam, Christianity considers the scriptures not the revelation itself but the original witness to the revelation.

These scriptural texts, therefore, serve as authority for Christian self-understanding by being authoritative witnesses to God's revelation in Jesus Christ. To say, "I believe in Jesus Christ with the apostles," is to mean that the religious, revelatory event of Jesus Christ experienced in the present Christian community is the same revelatory event witnessed by the original apostolic communities who wrote the New Testament. It is the revelatory event and not the witnessing texts that must play the central role in Christian self-understanding. Yet the 'book', the scriptures, plays a major theological role. For the scriptures are nothing less than the authoritative witness to that event—a witness to which all later Christian communities hold themselves accountable. To believe *in* Jesus Christ *with* the apostles means, for the Christian, that every present personal and communal Christian belief *in* Jesus Christ is in fundamental continuity with the apostolic witness expressed in the apostolic writings that have become the Christian New Testament. To believe in Jesus Christ, moreover, is to believe *in* the God of

Abraham, Isaac, and Jacob and thereby in the revelatory event of Sinai expressed in the Hebrew scriptures and reinterpreted as the Christian Old Testament in the light of the Christ-event witnessed to in the apostolic writings.

The complexities intrinsic to any Christian theological interpretation of the scriptures becomes clear. For Christianity is not a religion of the book, yet the book plays a central role in Christian self-understanding. Christianity, in more explicitly hermeneutical terms, is a religion of a revelatory event to which certain *texts* bear an authoritative witness.

It is difficult to exaggerate the importance of this distinction between event and text for Christian theological self-understanding. To fail to grasp the distinction is to lead into two opposite and familiar difficulties. To make the text into the revelation is to turn Christianity into a strict religion of the book on the model of the place of the Koran in Islam. Then the route to Christian fundamentalist readings of the scripture under the banner of "inerrancy" soon takes over. Here Christians believe, in effect, not *with* but *in* the apostles.

The opposite danger—removal of an authoritative role for the text in favor of a contemporary experience of the Christ-event alone—can be equally devastating for Christian self-understanding. It is not that such antitext positions are necessarily post-Christian. The difficulty is rather that, since the scriptural texts are not allowed to play any authoritative role, the contemporary Christian community can never know whether its present witness to the Christ-event is in continuity with the original apostolic witness. The historical central Christian theological affirmation, I believe in Jesus Christ with the apostles, has been narrowed into the sole affirmation, I believe in Jesus Christ.

Neither of these dangers has been present in the classic interpretation of the role of the Bible documented in earlier chapters. For despite their otherwise important, even radical, differences, all the classic mainline Christian interpreters maintained the hermeneutical distinction between the revelatory event of Jesus Christ and the scriptural texts that witness to that event. The text cannot replace the event to which it witnesses. Interpretation of the event as present in later Christian communities cannot ignore its own ap-

propriateness or lack of appropriateness to the authoritative witnessing apostolic texts. This has been the mainline Christian understanding of the role of text and event. This same position
informs and necessarily complicates Christian theological interpretation today.

It is worth noting that the scriptural texts themselves make the
same theological point. These texts are after all—as modern historical criticism has made clear—texts of witness by different
Christian communities to the event of Jesus Christ. In that precise
sense the scriptures of the New Testament are the church's book.

The New Testament texts, moreover, are by any reading remarkably diverse in both form and content. The contrast between
the genre of narrative in the Gospels and the genre of letters and
exhortations, the clash between Paul and James, the contrast between the tensive quality of the apocalyptic strands and the almost
relaxed stability of some of the Pastoral Epistles are differences
whose productive possibilities theologians and exegetes are still
investigating. What unites these remarkably pluralistic texts is not
any single interpretation of the Christ-event (any particular Christology) but the event itself. What unites them is the explicit belief
in Jesus Christ as revelation and the explicit fact of witness by the
early Christian communities to that event. In sum what unites the
New Testament is the Christian community's faith in Jesus Christ
as revelation. What unites later Christian communities to the early
community is contemporary faith in that same event of revelation.
What distinguishes the later communities' witness from that of the
early community is solely but critically the later communities' need
to show how necessary new interpretations of that revelatory
event are in appropriate continuity to the original witness to that
event. In short, what distinguishes the later communities is the presence of the earlier community's own witness as our scripture.

In this context, one cannot but affirm modern historical critical
studies of the scriptural texts. For these studies have clarified the
central theological points of the hermeneutical situation itself.
These methods have provided historico-critical reconstructions of
the original apostolic witnesses of the different communities (form
criticism) and different redactors (redaction criticism). They have
clarified both the different social settings (social science analysis)

and the diverse cultural settings (historical analysis) of these communities in relationship to their situation. By focusing, for example, on the import of such historical events as the destruction of Jerusalem (70 C.E.), the gentile mission, the persecution of the communities, the difficulties occasioned by the event which did not come (the end times), these historio-critical reconstructions have greatly clarified some of the situational reasons for the pluralism of interpretations of the Christ-event in the New Testament.

This remarkable modern series of historical critical clarifications of the situational pluralism of the early Christian communities has, in its turn, encouraged greater theological attentiveness to our own situational pluralism. That work has clarified anew the central insight that the scriptures are the church's book: They are products of and dependent upon the early Christian communities who composed them.

These insights can become the occasion, to be sure, to reduce the texts to the strictly historical events that they record. But if one keeps in mind the general rubrics for all interpretation and the general rubrics for theological interpretation, there is no sound reason why this reduction need occur.

Rather, theologically considered, historical reconstruction of the present biblical texts can be accorded full weight as reconstruction not of the situation alone but of the original apostolic witness to the Christ-event in a concrete situation. In principle there is no difference between the kind of situation-dependent interpretation of the Christ-event in the New Testament communities and the situation-dependent interpretation of that same event in the present Christian community. The only hermeneutical difference is one in fact. In fact contemporary Christian interpretation of the revelatory Christ-event must *also* show how its interpretation is appropriate to the interpretations of the original apostolic witnesses.

Some theologians (especially those in the Bultmannian school) also hold that the very pluralism of the New Testament interpretations of the Christ-event and the possibilities of reconstruction afforded by modern historical criticism impel Christian theologians to formulate new canons within the canon. Even those theologians like myself who do not share this belief in the need for a 'canon within the canon', do recognize that every theologian will in fact possess some 'working canon' for interpreting the pluralism of the New Testament. The studies of the methods of interpretation discussed in earlier chapters are eloquent testimony to the presence of such working canons throughout Christian history. There is, in short, need in theology as in every discipline for criteria of relative adequacy for poor or good or better readings of those different texts functioning as theological criteria of appropriateness to the scriptural witnesses to the Christ-event. Yet all such criteria need to be based on recognition of the relationship between text and event in Christian self-understanding. The central Christian belief remains the belief in Jesus Christ with the apostles. Which particular scriptural interpretation best expresses that belief and which contemporary Christian theological interpretation best expresses that same belief for our situation is *the* problem of Christian theological interpretation of the scriptures. Christian theology needs criteria of intelligibility for the situation and criteria of appropriateness to the scriptures, and needs to correlate both.

18

Theological Interpretation of the Scriptures in the Church: Prospect and Retrospect

It is time to summarize the results thus far by returning to the question of contemporary theological interpretation of the scriptures within the church, for in this issue the several strands of the argument may now meet. Let us recall those strands.

First, interpretation itself is a process best understood on the model of the conversation whereby the preunderstanding of the interpreter and the claim to attention of the text meet in that peculiar interaction called a conversation, where the subject matter itself takes over. This conversation should allow, moreover, for both hermeneutics of retrieval and of suspicion, for the use of both explanatory methods and understanding.

Second, theology is an interpretation that can be further classified by specifying the model of theological conversation as a correlation. Precisely as interpreter, every theologian attempts to interpret the scriptures by correlating an interpretation of the contemporary situation with an interpretation of the scriptural texts. This model of correlation is merely a heuristic one in order to clarify the intrinsically hermeneutical character of theology itself. The model clarifies by suggesting under the rubric of correlation the fuller spectrum of possible responses on any particular issue, from confrontation through similarity to identity. Correlation also clarifies the theological task by suggesting that theologians may further explicate their preunderstanding by providing specific interpretations of the principal religious question or questions in the contemporary situation.

The third and final strand of the argument suggests the fuller complexity of the theologian's task in interpreting scripture within the church: a recognition that these texts, by the church's own theological decision, have become the primary witnesses to the revelatory event of Jesus Christ. These texts witness to an event; they do not replace the event itself, nor are they simply replaceable by later concerns of later communities.

Such are the three major strands of our analysis. Together they yield the following picture of the theological interpretation of scripture within and for the church. There are, as stressed above, other interpreters of scripture within and for the church, and there are other modes of theological interpretation of the scriptures besides the one explicitly in and for the church community. We should recall, for example, that even if a theologian were not a believing member of the church community, he or she could still provide a theological interpretation of the scriptures so long as the religious questions of these biblical texts were allowed primacy in the conversation. In such a case we might speak of the theologian as providing a religious/theological interpretation of the Bible as classic religious texts with a claim to serious attention. But the theologian may often be a 'church theologian' in a stricter sense. As most of the theologians considered throughout this volume testify, the role of church theologian entails interpreting the scriptures as a believing member of the community for the community and in fidelity to the community's own norms.

This means that the theologian, like every other member of the believing community, accepts as normative the Christian belief in Jesus Christ with the apostles. This presumes the following facts: First, as a believer the theologian will appeal first to the presence of the revelatory Christ-event in her or his life. Thus does he or she say and mean, "I believe in Jesus Christ." Second, this personal faith is also recognized as mediated to an individual through the church community (both a concrete, local community and the abstract, centuries-old community of Christian tradition). Insofar as that recognition of the communal and traditional mediation of the Christ-event is present to the theologian, then she or he also affirms, with the mainline tradition, I believe in Jesus Christ *with the apostles*. At this point, a theologian recognizes his or her task as not merely to interpret the religious texts of the Bible but the scriptural texts—those texts chosen by the community as its own authoritative witness to the revelatory event of Jesus Christ. Now the explicitly theological interpretation of the scriptures as scriptures for the church community can begin.

That theological interpretation also will follow the rubrics of all good interpretation. In sum, the theologian will risk an interpretation of these scriptural texts. Their claim to attention will be theologically recognized by authoritative witnesses to the revelatory event—the same revelatory event present to the community now. As much as possible, moreover, the theologian will also endeavor to clarify the preunderstanding he or she brings to this conversation. That preunderstanding already includes a personal faith in Jesus Christ with the apostles; it may also include an explicit interpretation of some central religious questions in the concrete situation of the theologian's own culture and community.

Thus does the conversation begin. As the conversation proceeds it is likely that the de facto pluralism of the New Testament texts will provoke the theologian to formulate some working canon. That working canon at its best will prove faithful to the enriching pluralism of the interpretations and to the primary needs and questions of the contemporary community. Above all, the scriptural texts themselves will show that they, as original witnesses to the event, must be judged by the event itself. 'What is said' must be judged on the text's own grounds by 'what is meant'. For the fact is that both the tradition which mediates these texts within the present community and the texts themselves are often ambiguous. It remains crucial, therefore, to understand that the revelatory event must be allowed to judge the textual witnesses to the event. There is no sound scriptural or contemporary theological reason why any contemporary Christian need accept Paul's views on either women or slaves. (Indeed, an acceptance of Paul's own Christology should be sufficient to disallow those views.) There is no reason why any Christian today should not challenge the portrait of the Jews in John's Gospel and elsewhere in the New Testament. One may do so, moreover, not only on the basis of more accurate historical information about the Johannine communities and first-century Judaism, nor even on the basis of the frightening effects of these anti-Judaic texts in Christian anti-Semitism, but on the basis of the fundamental envisionment of all reality in Jesus Christ in John's own Gospel.

We find ourselves recognizing—now on inner Christian theological grounds—the need for hermeneutics of both retrieval and suspicion, the relevance of *any* explanatory method (historico-critical, literary critical, social scientific, ideology critique) which can aid the theological interpretation of these scriptural texts. The church tradition is and remains the major mediator of the Christ-event to the church community today. The church tradition, by its very choice of these particular texts as authoritative witnesses to the Christ-event, has released upon itself a powerful hermeneutics of both retrieval and suspicion which the scriptures express by their witness to that disorienting, jarring, revelatory event. It is not only our modern preunderstanding that demands the theological hermeneutics of retrieval and suspicion; it is the scriptures themselves. For there we learn to retrieve fully (as in John), to retrieve through suspicion (as in apocalypse), to retrieve and suspect all in the light of the revelatory event of Jesus Christ. The strangeness of the "strange, new world of the Bible" is experienced most concretely within the believing community itself. For there—when a conversation with the subject-matter event witnessed to by these texts is genuinely risked—there the disorienting power of these scriptural texts is felt with its fullest force. The Christian church, by its own commitment to these scriptural texts and the Christ-event to which they witness, must always risk allowing any corrective method, even any hermeneutics of suspicion which can clarify, purify, correct, and challenge its own traditional and present witness to those authoritative witnesses themselves.

As Ernst Troeltsch saw with clarity in the classic modern debate between Adolph von Harnack and Alfred Loisy, neither side (generically Protestant or Catholic) was entirely right or entirely wrong. With Loisy and the mainline Catholic tradition, one can and should recognize that it is the tradition which is our principal mediator of the event. The Bible is the church's book in three related senses: it comes to the present community through the mediation of past communities, the tradition; it comes to us as scripture because earlier church communities established a canon; it comes

to us, as modern historical criticism makes clear, as the witness of
the earliest church communities to the Christ-event. With Harnack
and the reformed tradition, all Christian theology should also recognize that the scriptures themselves and *a fortiori* the tradition
which mediates between them and us must always be viewed not
as the revelatory event itself but as texts and traditions witnessing
authoritatively to that event. All traditions—and even all scriptural
texts—must on their own inner Christian grounds allow themselves to judge what is said by what is meant. The event of Jesus
Christ judges the texts and traditions witnessing to it and not vice
versa.

It is, I believe, a profoundly Christian and scriptural act to trust
fundamentally in the tradition which mediates these scriptural texts
to us. To do so is to trust that the Spirit is present to the church in
spite of the church's errors. But such theological trust also suggests that there are errors both of mediation and of interpretation in
the tradition. A hermeneutics of retrieval—a hermeneutics, therefore, of fundamental trust—in the scriptures and the tradition
which mediates them to us is entirely appropriate in inner Christian
grounds. But a hermeneutics of real retrieval of the revelatory
event of Jesus Christ and the scriptural texts which witness to it
will always welcome every corrective, every explanatory method,
every hermeneutics of suspicion that can aid the tradition to maintain and purify its trust. Theological interpretations that risk such
conversation are one means by which the church attempts to maintain its trust.

And every other kind of interpretation of the scriptures that allows the religious questions of these texts to become the questions
of the interpreter should be recognized within the church as aiding
its own deepest concern. Historico-critical, social scientific, literary
critical, rhetorical, philosophical, nonbelieving theological analyses of the biblical texts all aid the church's self-interpretation by
the church's own scriptural standards. For any interpretation which
allows these biblical texts to become genuinely religious texts in
interpretation as conversation also aids the church for whom these
religious texts have become scripture.

A major part of the tradition of the church is, of course, precisely the tradition studied in earlier chapters. Contemporary theol-

ogy lives on the heritage of those earlier methods of interpretation. Each classic method fulfilled in its time the same effort at interpretation of the scriptures for its contemporary situation that theology attempts for our day. Each of these classic models also correlated an interpretation of the scriptures with an interpretation of contemporary religious questions. Each tradition of interpretation, beginning with Paul's Christocentric focus and the use of typology in Hebrews, developed classic ways to retrieve the significance of the revelation event for later times.

Every classic is particular in both origin and expression yet public, even transcultural, in effect. The effect of every classic discloses both an excess and a permanence of meaning that later generations must retrieve. Contemporary theology continues to learn from Paul and Hebrews, indeed from all the classic genres of interpretation in both Testaments. Contemporary theology also continues to learn from the need for intelligibility to a given situation disclosed in the daring development of allegorical methods begun in Alexandria. We continue to learn from the emphasis on the primacy of the literal sense in Antioch, in Thomas Aquinas, and in Luther. Theologians continue to learn the import of the phrase 'with the apostles' and the significance of tradition from further reflection on Irenaeus and other classic exponents of the 'authoritative' (not authoritarian) model.

Yet, as this work has shown, really to learn from these classic ways of interpreting scriptures is to hold genuine conversation with them. As their *conversation* partners we must note their just claim to our attention, and we must ask critical questions of each of them and of ourselves. To commit oneself to a hermeneutics of full retrieval is also to engage in a hermeneutics of critique and suspicion of the classic ways of traditional interpretation.

This rubric is simply a contemporary way of saying that the Christian church lives by allowing the full dialectic of faith, scripture, tradition, and reason. Every classic tradition lives as *traditio,* not mere *tradita,* if all the requirements of a conversation with its classics are to be satisfied. The models of scriptural interpretation studied throughout this work live today as classics. They can neither be forgotten nor simply repeated. They must be interpreted— conversed with in the same spirit of seriousness which impelled their own labors of interpretation. No more than the other classics—of Plato, Aristotle, Dante, Michelangelo, Shakespeare, etc.—will the scriptures ever receive a definitive, once-and-for-all interpretation. Each generation must struggle to understand them anew. And each generation can do so with integrity by entering into the centuries-old classic history of conversations with the scriptures which these chapters have documented. To understand at all is to understand in conversation with all the classic attempts to interpret the scriptures from Jesus and Paul to our own day.

Notes

CHAPTER 1

1. W. Dilthey, *Gesammelte Schriften,* 5:278; in H. A. Hodges, *Wilhelm Dilthey: An Introduction* (New York, 1944), 128; reprinted by permission of the Oxford University Press, New York.

CHAPTER 2

1. Sanhedrin 99a; B. H. Branscomb, *Jesus and the Law of Moses* (New York, 1930), 156.

2. E. v. Dobschütz, "Matthäus als Rabbi und Katechet," *Zeitschrift für die neutestamentliche Wissenschaft* 27 (1928): 338–48.

3. J. Bonsirven, *Exégèse rabbinique et exégèse paulinienne* (Paris, 1939), 24.

4. W. Manson, *Jesus the Messiah* (Philadelphia, 1946), 229 ff.

5. B. T. D. Smith, *S. Matthew* (Cambridge, 1926), 96; Branscomb, *Jesus and the Law,* 216.

6. Sifre Deut. 49 end, cited by G. F. Moore, *Judaism in the Age of the Tannaim* (Cambridge, 1927), 1:319, n. 4.

7. Moore, *Judaism,* 319; reprinted by permission of the Harvard University Press.

8. E. Klostermann, *Jesu Stellung zum Alten Testament* (Kiel, 1904), 28.

CHAPTER 3

1. See my note in *Harvard Theological Review* 39 (1946): 71 ff.

2. It should be observed that Deut. 25:4 is entirely unrelated to its context. Thus the idea of a hidden meaning could arise, as in the case of Melchizedek.

3. Pseudo-Heraclitus, *Quaestiones homericae,* 6.

4. Bonsirven, *Exégèse rabbinique,* 309 f.

5. Cf. W. Morgan, *The Religion and Theology of Paul* (Edinburgh, 1917), 3 ff.; E. Stauffer, *Die Theologie des Neuen Testaments* (Geneva, 1945), 3 ff.

6. Bonsirven, *Exégèse rabbinque,* 298 f. When Paul repeats his ar-

gument about the promise in Romans 4, he does not interpret "seed" in this way.

7. O. Michel, *Paulus und seine Bibel* (Gütersloh, 1929), 29.

8. Ibid., 178 f.

9. C. F. Burney, "Christ as the APXH of Creation," *Journal of Theological Studies* 27 (1925–26): 160 ff.

10. Bonsirven, *Exégèse rabbinique*, 307; cf. Philo, *Paen.* 183.

11. Michel, *Paulus*, 111. Cf. W. L. Knox, *Some Hellenistic Elements in Primitive Christianity* (London, 1944), 34 ff.

CHAPTER 4

1. E. F. Scott, *The Epistle to the Hebrews* (New York, 1922), 53; reprinted by permission of Charles Scribner's Sons. On the exegesis of Hebrews see P. Lestringant, *Essai sur l'unité de la révélation biblique* (Paris, 1942), 127 ff.

2. G. Wuttke, *Melchisedek der Priesterkönig von Salem* (Giessen, 1927), 3 ff.

3. R. Hanson, "Moses in the Typology of St. Paul," *Theology* 48 (1945): 174 ff.; Hebrews 3; I. Lévy, *La légende de Pythagore* (Paris, 1927), 334 f.

4. H. Strack and P. Billerbeck, *Kommentar zum Neuen Testament aus Talmud und Midrasch* (München, 1922), 1:78.

5. P. Lestringant, *Essai sur l'unité de la révélation biblique* (Paris, 1942), 117 f.

6. F. J. A. Hort, *Judaistic Christianity* (London, 1894), 130 ff. An example of such "Jewish" interpretations is the work of Papias of Hierapolis; see Jerome, *De viris inlustribus* 18; J. R. Harris in *American Journal of Theology* 2 (1900): 499.

7. A modern attempt to uphold this method is L. Goppelt, *Typos: die typologische Deutung des Alten Testaments im Neuen* (Gütersloh, 1939), especially 1–21.

8. *Die Theologie des Neuen Testaments* (Geneva, 1945), 234. See also ch. 8.

CHAPTER 5

1. H. Windisch, *Der Barnabasbrief* (Tübingen, 1920), 395.

2. Barnabas 9:8. The number 318 means Jesus, because in Greek *TIH* make up the cross plus the first two letters of Jesus' name.

3. J. Knox, *Marcion and the New Testament* (Chicago, 1942); but see *The Letter and the Spirit* (London, 1957), 115–19.

4. E. R. Goodenough, *The Theology of Justin Martyr* (Jena, 1925).

5. *Apol.* 1.1, 26 Goodsp.; cf. *Dial.* 120.6, 240; P. R. Weis, "Some Samaritanisms of Justin Martyr," *Journal of Theological Studies* 45 (1944): 199 ff.

6. A. Harnack, *Sitzungsberichte d. preuss. Akad. d. Wiss.*, 1902.

7. "The Decalogue in Early Christianity," *Harvard Theological Review* 40 (1947): 1 ff.

8. P. de Labriolle, *La réaction paienne*, 7th ed. (Paris, 1942), 119.

9. N. Bonwetsch, *Die Theologie des Irenäus* (Gütersloh, 1925); J. Hoh, *Die Lehre des Hl. Irenäus über das Neue Testament* (Münster, 1919), 86–117.

10. A. Harnack, "Die Presbyter-Prediger bei Irenäus," *Philotesia* (Berlin, 1907), 1 ff.

11. See ch. 8.

CHAPTER 6

1. C. Siegfried, *Philo von Alexandria als Ausleger des Alten Testaments* (Jena, 1875); P. Heinisch, *Der Einfluss Philos auf die älteste christliche Exegese* (Münster, 1908); H.A. Wolfson, *Philo,* vols. 1–2 (Cambridge, Mass., 1947).

2. W. Bousset, *Jüdisch-Christlicher Schulbetrieb in Alexandria und Rom* (Göttingen, 1915), 8.

3. Heinisch, *Der Einfluss,* 67 ff.

4. On Gnostics and their exegesis see R. M. Grant, *Gnosticism and Early Christianity* (New York, 1959).

5. W. Foerster, *Von Valentinus zu Heracleon* (Giessen, 1928).

6. C. Mondésert, *Clément d' Alexandrie* (Paris, 1944), 153 ff.

7. Ibid., 97 ff.

8. F. Prat, *Origène, le théologue et l'exégéte* (Paris, 1907), 111 ff.; A. Zöllig, *Die Inspirationslehre de Origenes* (Freiburg, 1902), 91 ff.

9. Prat, *Origène,* 127 ff., 175 ff.; Zöllig, *Die Inspirationslehre,* 102 ff.

10. Zöllig, *Die Inspirationslehre,* 96.

11. Ibid., 96 f.; cf. *De Pr.* 1. praef. 4 (11:10 K); 4.2.2 (308:15).

CHAPTER 7

1. See J. Forget, "Jerome (Saint)," *Dictionnaire de théologie catholique* (Paris, 1924), 8:962; A. Vaccari, "I fattori della esegesi geronomiana," *Biblica* 1 (1920): 457 ff.

2. C. H. Kraeling, "The Jewish Community of Antioch," *Journal of Biblical Literature* 51 (1932): 130 ff.; A. Marmorstein in *The Expositor,* Eighth Series 17 (1919), 104 ff.; Eusebius, *HE* 7.32.2.

3. H. B. Swete, *Theodori Episcopi Mopsuesteni in epistolas B. Pauli*

Commentarii (Cambridge, 1880), 1:74 ff.

4. J.-M. Vosté, "L'oeuvre exégétique de Théodore de Mopsueste au iie concile de Constantinople," *Revue biblique* 38 (1929): 544 ff.

5. But cf. R. Devreesse, *Le commentaire de Théodore de Mopsueste sur les Psaumes* (Rome, 1939), xxix.

6. Ibid., 547.

7. A. Vaccari, "La ΘΕΩΡΙΑ nella scuola esegetica di Antiochia," *Biblica* 1 (1920): 14.

8. *In Isa.* 5, Migne PG 56, 60.

9. Vaccari, "La ΘΕΩΡΙΑ," 1 ff.; L. Pirot, *L'oeuvre exégétique de Théodore de Mopsueste* (Rome, 1913), 177 ff.

10. Vosté, "L'oeuvre," 542 ff.; Pirot, "L'oeuvre," 235 ff.; Devreesse, *Le commentaire*, 120 ff.

11. L. Dennefeld, *Der Alttestamentliche Kanon der antiochenischen Schule* (Freiburg, 1909), 44 ff.

12. Vosté, "L'oeuvre," 394 f.

13. H. Kihn, *Theodor von Mopsuestia und Junilius Africanus als Exegeten* (Freiburg, 1880), 75 f.

14. Vosté, "L'oeuvre," 388 f.

15. *In Epist. ad. Gal. comm.*, Migne PG 61, 662.

16. *In Epist. ad Phil. hom.* 10, Migne PG 62, 257; cf. Heb. 10:1; Melito, *Homily on the Passion* 36–38 (107 ff. Bonner).

17. K. K. Hulley, "Principles of Textual Criticism Known to St. Jerome," *Harvard Studies in Classical Philology* 55 (1944): 87 ff.

18. Augustine, *Ep.* 71; CSEL 34, 248 ff.; Pirot, "L'oeuvre," 102.

19. See Vaccari, "I fattori."

20. F. Goessling, *Adrians* ΕΙΣΑΓΩΤΗ ΕΙΣ ΤΑΣ ΘΕΙΑΣΓΡΑΦΑΣ (Berlin, 1887), 13.

21. Ibid., 130 ff.

22. Kihn, *Theodor von Mopsuestia*, 213 ff.; cf. T. Hermann, "Die Schule von Nisibis vom 5. bis 7. Jahrhundert," *Zeitschrift für die neutestamentliche Wissenschaft* 25 (1926): 89 ff.

23. M. L. Laistner, "Antiochene Exegesis in Western Europe during the Middle Ages," *Harvard Theological Review* 40 (1947): 9 ff.

24. Pirot, "L'oeuvre," 121 ff.; Junilius, 1, 3 ff.

CHAPTER 8

1. N. Bonwetsch, *Die Theologie des Methodius von Olympus* (Göttingen, 1903), 147.

2. Tertullian, *De praesc.* 15; cf. "The Bible in the Ancient Church," *Journal of Religion* 26 (1946): 190 ff.

3. *De Praesc.* 19.

4. *Inst. orat.* 7.5; J.-L. Allie, *L'argument de préscription dans le droit romain, en apologétique, et en théologie dogmatique* (Ottawa, 1940), 49.

5. *La théologie de Tertullian* (Paris, 1905), 247; G. Zimmermann, *Die hermeneutischen Prinzipien Tertullians* (Würzburg, 1937), 11.

6. C. Mondésert, *Clément d'Alexandrie* (Paris, 1944), 148 ff.

7. Methodius, *Sympos.* 7.7 (89:3 Bonwetsch).

8. *De lepra* 13.2 (467:23).

9. Bonwetsch, *Die Theologie,* 143 ff.

10. Augustine, *Conf.* 3.7.12.

11. Ibid., 5.11.21.

12. P. de Labriolle, "Saint Ambroise et l'exégèse allégorique," *Annales de philos. chrét.* 155 (1908), 591 ff.

13. *Conf.* 6.4.6.

14. *De doctr. christ.* 1.36.40.

15. Ibid., 3.2. In 3.5 he calls it the *praescriptio fidei.*

16. Ibid., Prol. 2.

17. Vincent, *Common,* 2. (2), 3:17 Jülicher.

18. Ibid., 4, 4 f.

19. Ibid., 10 (15), 13 f.

20. Ibid., 17 f., 25 ff.

21. Ibid., 21 (26), 31:30. Vincent uses a Latin version.

22. Ibid., 23 (30), 35:23.

23. Ibid., 25 f., 39 ff.

24. A. Jülicher, *Vincenz von Lerinum,* 2d ed. Tübingen, 1925), x f.

25. Vincent, *Common.* 18 (24), 28:29.

26. Allie, *L'argument,* 122 n.4.

27. Vincent, *Common.* 6 (9), 8:19.

28. Migne, *Patrol. Lat.* 210, 245.

29. E. Mangenot and J. Rivière, "Interprétation de l'Ecriture," *Dictionnaire de Théologie Catholique* (Paris, 1923), 7:2294 ff., 2321.

CHAPTER 9

1. Vincent of Lerins, *Common.* 2 (2), 3 Jülicher. On catenas see G. Heinrici, "Catenae," *New Schaff-Herzog Encyclopedia,* 2:451 ff.; R. Devreesse, "Chaînes exégétiques grecques," *Dictionnaire de la bible, Suppl.* 1 (Paris, 1928).

2. B. Smalley, *The Study of the Bible in the Middle Ages* (Oxford, 1941), 31 ff., 156 ff. Quotations are made by permission of the Clarendon Press.

3. Cassiodorus, *Institutiones* 1.10.1, 34 Mynors.

4. R. A. B. Mynors, *Cassiodori Senatoris Institutiones* (Oxford, 1937), xxii.

5. On the circulation of Junilius Africanus see M. L. W. Laistner as cited ch. 7, n. 23.

6. L. Ginzberg, *Die Haggada bei den Kirchenväter* (Berlin, 1900); S. Krauss in *Jewish Encyclopedia*, 4:80 ff., 115 ff.

7. Smalley, *Study of the Bible*, 86 ff.

8. Ibid., 105.

9. Ibid., 134.

10. E. Mangenot, "'Almah," *Dictionnaire de la bible* (Paris, 1891), 1:394 f.

11. E. v. Dobschütz, "Vom vierfachen Schriftsinn," *Harnack-Ehrung* (Leipzig, 1921), 1 ff.; H. Caplan, "The Four Senses of Scriptural Interpretation," *Speculum* 4 (1929): 282 ff.

12. v. Dobschütz, "Vom vierfachen Schriftsinn," 3.

13. Smalley, *Study of the Bible*, 218.

14. See D. L. Douie, *The Nature and the Effect of the Heresy of the Fraticelli* (Manchester, 1932), 22 ff.

15. Smalley, *Study of the Bible*, 217.

16. *Summa theologica* 1.1.8. See E. Gilson, *Reason and Revelation in the Middle Ages* (New York, 1938).

17. *S.T.* 1.1.9.

18. *S.T.* 1.1.10; see also *Quodl.* 7. a. 14–16; P. Synave, "La doctrine de St. Thomas d'Aquin sur le sens littéral des Ecritures," *Revue biblique* 35 (1926): 40 ff.; other references in V. J. Bourke, *Thomistic Bibliography 1920–1940* (St. Louis, 1945), 244 ff.

19. See J. M. Heald, "Aquinas," *Encyclopaedia of Religion and Ethics*, 1:659.

CHAPTER 10

1. Weimar edition, 2:279; quoted by J. Mackinnon, *Luther and the Reformation* (London-New York, 1930), 4:296.

2. See M. Reu, *Luther's German Bible* (Columbus, 1934).

3. *Tischreden*, Weimar edition, 1:136; quoted by K. Holl, "Luthers Bedeutung für den Fortschritt der Auslegungskunst," *Gesammelte Aufsätze zur Kirchengeschichte* (Tübingen, 1921), 1:420.

4. Erlangen edition, 46, 338 f.; quoted by K. Fullerton, "Luther's Doctrine and Criticism of Scripture," *Bibliotheca Sacra* 63 (1906), 8.

5. Weimar edition, 5, 108; Mackinnon, *Luther*, 4:293.

6. Holl, *Tischreden*, 445.

7. Fullerton, "Luther's Doctrine," 16.

8. Ibid., 12.

9. *Exposition of the 37th (36th) Psalm;* Mackinnon, *Luther,* 294 f.

10. Fullerton, "Luther's Doctrine," 18.

11. *Inst.* 3.5.5. On Calvin's exegesis see J. Mackinnon, *Calvin and the Reformation* (New York, 1936), 220 ff.

12. *Inst.* 1.7. These quotations are taken from chapters 7 and 8.

13. K. Fullerton, *Prophecy and Authority* (New York, 1919), 150 ff.

14. *Tischreden,* 1:108; Mackinnon, *Luther,* 4:284.

15. Fullerton, *Prophecy,* 165 ff.; cf. M. Reu, *Luther and the Scriptures* (Columbus, 1944), 117 ff.

16. Book 2, hom. 10.

17. S. E. Johnson, "The Episcopal Church and the Bible," *Anglican Theological Review* 24 (1942): 310 f. Note the literalism of Martin Bucer: A. Lang, *Der Evangelienkommentar Martin Butzers* (Leipzig, 1900), 35 ff.; S. Brown-Serman in A. C. Zabriskie, *Anglican Evangelicalism* (Philadelphia, 1943), 80 ff.

18. See E. Cailliet, *The Clue to Pascal* (Philadelphia, 1943), 67.

19. Pensées, frag. 278 Brunschwicg; H. F. Stewart, *Pascal's Apology for Religion* (Cambridge, 1942), 190, frag. 608.

20. Frag. 578 Br., 497 Stewart (p. 158).

21. Frag. 684 Br., 503 Stewart (p. 160).

22. Cailliet, *The Clue,* 154 ff.

23. H. T. Kerr, Jr., *A Compend of Luther's Theology* (Philadelphia, 1943), 14; Weimar ed., 18:1588.

24. Ibid., 17; Weimar ed., 6:509.

25. P. Lehmann, "The Reformers' Use of the Bible," *Theology Today* 3 (1946): 328 ff.

CHAPTER 11

1. J. A. Froude, *Life and Letters of Erasmus* (New York, 1948), 141.

2. Ibid., 48.

3. J. H. Lupton, *Life of Dean Colet* (London, 1887), 106.

4. J. M. Robertson, *A Short History of Freethought* (London, 1915), 2:5 f.

5. See J. Mackinnon, *The Origins of the Reformation* (London, 1939), 359 f.

6. F. W. Farrar, *History of Interpretation* (London, 1886), 373 ff. Yet note that the phrase "pens of the Holy Spirit" comes from Augustine (*Conf.* 7.21.27, CSEL 33, 166).

7. *Ecclesiastical Polity* 2.8.1; see P. E. More and F. L. Cross, *Angli-*

canism (Milwaukee, 1935), 89 ff.; compare the attitude of the Presbyterian John Owen (J. C. Dana, "John Owen's Conception and Use of the Bible" [Presbyterian Theological Seminary B.D. thesis, 1941], 46 ff.). I am grateful to Professor G. E. Wright for this point.

8. Robertson, *Freethought,* 35, 95, 133.

9. H. Margival, *Essai sur Richard Simon et la critique biblique au xviie siècle* (Paris, 1900).

10. Robertson, *Freethought,* 116; cf. Luke 18:8.

CHAPTER 12

1. See "Historical Criticism in the Ancient Church," *Journal of Religion* 25 (1945): 183 ff.; J. Geffcken, "Zur Entstehung und zum Wesen des griechischen wissenschaftlichen Kommentars," *Hermes* 67 (1932), 397–412.

2. H. F. Hutson, "Some Factors in the Rise of Scientific New Testament Criticism," *Journal of Religion* 22 (1942): 89 ff.

3. J. Wach, *Das Verstehen, Grundzüge einer Geschichte der hermeneutischen Theorie im 19. Jahrhundert* (Tübingen, 1926), 1:121 ff.

4. F. Lichtenberger, *History of German Theology in the Nineteenth Century* (Eng. trans., Edinburgh, 1889), 116, 137.

5. Especially his analysis of the epistles to Timothy.

6. Lichtenberger, *History,* 18 ff.

7. C. C. McCown, *The Search for the Real Jesus* (New York, 1940), 87 ff.; A. Schweitzer, *Von Reimarus zu Wrede* (Tübingen, 1906), pays too little attention to him. See the articles in various journals by Dr. Mary Andrews.

8. To say that this exegesis gives "opportunities for obscurantist dogmatism" (McCown, *Search,* 48) is to neglect the dogmatism of Baur and Strauss.

9. E. C. Vanderlaan, *Protestant Modernism in Holland* (London, 1924).

10. Ibid., 31 ff.

11. Ibid., 99 ff.

12. E. Renan, *Souvenirs d'enfance et de jeunesse* (Paris: Nelson, 1938), 224 f.

13. McCown, *Search,* 73.

14. C. R. Sanders, *Coleridge and the Broad Church Movement* (Duke, 1942), 51.

15. *Table Talk of Samuel Taylor Coleridge,* ed. H. Morley (London, 1884), 37 f. (January 6, 1823).

16. Ibid., 69 (April 17, 1830).

17. Ibid., 147 (March 31, 1832).

18. Ibid., 212 (June 15, 1833).

19. Sanders, *Coleridge*, 98.

20. Ibid., 258; see J. S. Marshall, "Philosophy Through Exegesis," *Anglican Theological Review* 26 (1944): 204 ff.

21. See H. P. Smith, *Essays in Biblical Interpretation* (Boston, 1921), 128 ff. Mention should also be made of the Scottish trial of W. Robertson Smith.

22. *God and the Bible* (New York, 1903), 39 f.

23. L. Trilling, *Matthew Arnold* (New York, 1939), 332 f.

24. For example, Keble in *Tracts for the Times*, no. 89, and Newman, no. 90.

25. See the articles on them by W. F. Albright in *Dictionary of American Biography*, 18:174 f., 16:39 f. I owe these references to Professor G. E. Wright.

26. J. Coppens, *The Old Testament and the Critics* (Eng. trans., Paterson, N.J., 1942), 30 f.; reprinted by permission of the St. Anthony's Guild Press. Cf. J. Wellhausen, *Prolegomena to the History of Israel* (Eng. trans., Edinburgh, n.d.); W. F. Albright, *From the Stone Age to Christianity* (Baltimore, 1940), 52 f., 244. A modification of Wellhausen's view is defended in R. H. Pfeiffer's important *Introduction to the Old Testament* (New York, 1941).

27. *What is Christianity?* (Eng. trans., London, 1901), 51.

28. Ibid., 13 f.

29. Ibid., 278.

30. "The Christ that Harnack sees, looking back through nineteen centuries of Catholic darkness, is only the reflection of a liberal Protestant face seen at the bottom of a deep well" (G. Tyrrell, *Christianity at the Cross-Roads* [London, 1909], 44).

CHAPTER 13

1. Renan, *Souvenirs*, 133.

2. Ibid., 158.

3. Ibid., 213; cf. W. M. Macgregor, *Persons and Ideals* (Edinburgh, 1939), 92 ff.

4. A. Vidler, *The Modernist Movement in the Roman Church* (Cambridge, 1934), 60 ff.

5. See A. Houtin, *La question biblique chez les catholiques de France aux xixe siècle* (Paris, 1902).

6. *The Gospel and the Church*, 2d ed. (New York, 1909), 13.

7. Ibid., 219.

8. M. D. Petre, *Alfred Loisy* (Cambridge, 1944), 17.

9. See Vidler, *Modernist Movement.*, 69 ff.

10. See H. R. Niebuhr, *The Meaning of Revelation* (New York, 1941).

11. Coppens, *Old Testament*, 139 ff.

12. See Vidler, *Modernist Movement*, 217 ff.

13. *Vivre et Penser* 3 (1943–44): 7.

CHAPTER 14

1. A. Schweitzer (Eng. trans., New York, 1933), 16.

2. H. J. Ebeling, *Das Messiasgeheimnis und die Botschaft des Marcus-Evangelisten* (Berlin, 1939).

3. E. Schwartz, *Fünf Vorträge über den griechischen Roman* (Berlin, 1896), 7 ff.

4. J. Coppens, *Old Testament,* 50 ff. Cf. G. E. Wright, "Neo-Orthodoxy and the Bible," *Journal of Bible and Religion* 14 (1946): 87 ff.; "Interpreting the Old Testament," *Theology Today* 3 (1946): 176 ff.; "Biblical Archaeology Today," *The Biblical Archaeologist* 10 (1947): 7 ff.

5. L. Salvatorelli, "From Locke to Reitzenstein," *Harvard Theological Review* 22 (1929): 263 ff.; see A. D. Nock, *Conversion* (Oxford, 1933); *St. Paul* (London, 1938).

6. H. J. Cadbury, *The Peril of Modernizing Jesus* (New York, 1937); Ebeling, *Das Messiasgeheimnis*, 95 ff., 220 ff.; M. Dibelius, *Gospel Criticism and Christology* (London, 1935); F. C. Grant, *Frontiers of Christian Thinking* (Chicago, 1935), 37 ff.

7. The method has been applied to the epistolary literature of the New Testament by P. Carrington, *The Primitive Christian Catechism* (Cambridge, 1940); cf. E. G. Selwyn, *The First Epistle of St. Peter* (London, 1946), 363 ff.

8. *Zeitschrift für Theologie und Kirche* 54 (1957): 279–80.

9. K. Barth, *The Word of God and the Word of Man,* trans. Douglas Horton (Boston, 1928); idem., *The Doctrine of the Word of God* (New York, 1936), 98 ff.

10. *Word of God and the Word of Man,* 60; reprinted by permission of the Pilgrim Press.

11. Ibid., 74; reprinted by permission of the Pilgrim Press.

CHAPTER 15

1. "The Problem of Hermeneutics," *Essays Philosophical and Theological* (New York, 1955), 234–61.

Select English Bibliography

I. GENERAL

Barr, J. *Old and New in Interpretation: A Study of the Two Testaments.* New York, 1966.

———. *The Semantics of Biblical Language.* New York, 1960.

The Cambridge History of the Bible. 3 vols. Cambridge, 1963–70.

Colwell, E. C. *The Study of the Bible.* Chicago, 1937.

Dobschütz, E. von. "Interpretation." *Encyclopedia of Religion and Ethics* VII, p. 390.

Dugmore, C. W., ed. *The Interpretation of the Bible.* London, 1944.

Farrar, F. W. *History of Interpretation.* London, 1886.

Gilbert, G. H. *Interpretation of the Bible.* New York, 1908.

Grant, R. M. *A Historical Introduction to the New Testament.* New York, 1963.

McKim, D. K., ed. *The Authoritative Word: Essays on the Nature of Scripture.* Grand Rapids, 1983.

Smart, James D. *The Interpretation of Scripture.* Philadelphia, 1961.

Smith, H. P. *Essays in Biblical Interpretation.* Boston, 1921.

II. HERMENEUTICS

Gadamer, Hans-Georg. *Philosophical Hermeneutics.* Berkeley, 1976.

———. *Truth and Method.* New York, 1975.

Habermas, Jürgen. *Knowledge and Human Interests.* Boston, 1971.

Howard, Roy J. *Three Faces of Hermeneutics.* Berkeley, 1982.

Jauss, Hans Robert. *Toward an Aesthetic of Reception.* Minneapolis, 1982.

Palmer, Richard. *Hermeneutics: Interpretation Theory in Schleiermacher, Dilthey, Heidegger and Gadamer*. Evanston, 1969.

Ricoeur, Paul. *Interpretation Theory*. Fort Worth, 1976.

Said, Edward W. *The World, the Text and the Critic*. Cambridge, 1983.

III. ANCIENT AND MEDIEVAL

Bate, H. N. "Some Technical Terms of Greek Exegesis." *Journal of Theological Studies* 24 (1922–23): 59.

Branscomb, B. H. *Jesus and the Law of Moses*. New York, 1930.

Chase, G. H. *Chrysostom: A Study in the History of Biblical Interpretation*. Cambridge, 1887.

Daniélou, J. *The Bible and the Liturgy*. Notre Dame, Ind., 1956.

———. *From Shadows to Reality: Studies in the Biblical Typology of the Fathers*. Westminster, Md., 1960.

———. *Origen*. New York, 1955.

Davies, W. D. *Paul and Rabbinic Judaism*. London, 1948.

Fahey, M. A. *Cyprian and the Bible: A Study in Third Century Exegesis*. Tübingen, 1971.

Gilson, E. *Reason and Revelation in the Middle Ages*. New York, 1938.

Grant, R. M. *The Earliest Lives of Jesus*. London and New York, 1961.

———. *Early Christianity and Society: Seven Studies*. New York, 1977.

———. *The Letter and the Spirit*. London, 1957.

Hanson, R. P. C. *Allegory and Event*. London, 1959.

Knox, J. *Marcion and the New Testament*. Chicago, 1942.

Lampe, G. W. H., and K. J. Woollcombe. *Essays on Typology*. Naperville, Ill., 1957.

Lawson, J. *The Biblical Theory of St. Irenaeus*. London, 1948.

Moore, G. F. *Judaism in the Age of the Tannaim I–III*. Cambridge, Mass., 1927–30.

Robbins, F. E. *The Hexaemeral Literature*. Chicago, 1912.

Smalley, B. *The Study of the Bible in the Middle Ages*. 2d ed. Oxford, 1952.

Smith, H. *Ante-Nicene Exegesis of the Gospels I–VI*. London, 1925–29.

Tasker, R. V. G. *The Old Testament in the New Testament*. Philadelphia, 1947.

Tollinton, R. B. *Selections from the Commentaries and Homilies of Origen*. London, 1929.

Wolfson, H. A. *Philo I–II*. Cambridge, Mass., 1947.

IV. REFORMATION

Fullerton, K. *Prophecy and Authority*. New York, 1919.

Mackinnon, J. *Calvin and the Reformation*. London, 1936.

———. *Luther and the Reformation IV*. New York and London, 1930.

Pelikan, J. J. *Luther the Expositor*. St. Louis, 1959.

Reu, M. *Luther's German Bible*. Columbus, Ohio, 1934.

———. *Luther and the Scriptures*. Columbus, Ohio, 1944.

Stewart, H. F. *Pascal's Apology for Religion*. Cambridge, 1942.

Tavard, G. *Holy Writ or Holy Church*. London, 1959.

V. RENAISSANCE AND MODERN

Albright, W. F. *From the Stone Age to Christianity*. Baltimore, 1940.

Barr, J. *The Scope and Authority of the Bible*. Philadelphia, 1980.

Barth, K. *The Word of God and the Word of Man*. Boston, 1928.

Beardslee, William. *Literary Criticism of the New Testament*. Philadelphia, 1970.

Bultmann, R. *Essays Philosophical and Theological*. New York, 1955.

———. "Is Exegesis without Presuppositions Possible?" and "The Problem of Hermeneutics." In *Existence and Faith*, edited by Schubert Ogden. New York, 1964.

———. *Theology of the New Testament*. 2 vols. New York, 1953.

Cadbury, H. J. *The Peril of Modernizing Jesus*. New York, 1937.

Childs, Brevard S. *Biblical Theology in Crisis*. Philadelphia, 1970.

———. *Introduction to the Old Testament as Scripture*. Philadelphia, 1979.

Cobb, John, and James Robinson, eds. *The New Hermeneutic*. New York, 1964.

Coppens, J. *The Old Testament and the Critics*. Paterson, N.J., 1942.

Craig, C. T. "Biblical Theology and the Rise of Historicism." *Journal of Biblical Literature* 62 (1943): 281.

Crossman, J. Dominic. *Cliffs of Fall: Paradox and Polyvalence in the Parables of Jesus*. New York, 1980.

Cunliffe-Jones, H. *The Authority of the Biblical Revelation*. London, 1945.

Dibelius, M. *Gospel Criticism and Christology*. London, 1935.

Dodd, C. H. *The Authority of the Bible*. London, 1928.

———. *History and the Gospel*. New York, 1938.

Frei, Hans. *The Eclipse of Biblical Narrative: A Study in Eighteenth and Nineteenth Century Hermeneutics*. New Haven, 1974.

Funk, Robert W. *Language, Hermeneutics and the Word of God*. New York, 1966.

Green, V. H. H. *Bishop Reginald Pecock*. Cambridge, 1945.

Harnack, A. von. *What Is Christianity?* New York, 1901.

Kermode, Frank. *The Genesis of Secrecy: On the Interpretation of Narrative*. Cambridge, Mass., 1979.

Knox, J. *Criticism and Faith*. New York, 1952.

Kümmel, W. G. *The New Testament: The History of the Investigation of Its Problems*. Translated by S. McL. Gilmour and H. C. Kee. Nashville, 1972.

Lichtenberger, F. *History of German Theology in the Nineteenth Century*. Edinburgh, 1889.

Loisy, A. *The Gospel and the Church*. Translated by C. Home. New York, 1912.

McCown, C. C. *The Search for the Real Jesus*. New York, 1940.

Minear, P. S. *Eyes of Faith*. 1946.

Nash, H. S. *The History of the Higher Criticism of the New Testament*. New York, 1900.

Ogden, Schubert. *Christ without Myth*. New York, 1961.

Perrin, Norman. *Jesus and the Language of the Kingdom: Symbol and Metaphor in New Testament Interpretation*. Philadelphia, 1976.

Ricoeur, Paul. "Biblical Hermeneutics." *Semeia* 4: 29–148. (The journal *Semeia* has taken the lead in publishing articles in the various approaches to biblical hermeneutics.)

Robinson, J. M. *A New Quest of the Historical Jesus*. Naperville, Ill., 1959.

Salvatorelli, L. "From Locke to Reitzenstein." *Harvard Theological Review* 22 (1929): 263.

Schubert, P. "New Testament Study and Theology." *Religion in Life* 14 (1945): 556.

Smart, J. D. "The Death and Rebirth of Old Testament Theology." *Journal of Religion* 23 (1943): I, 125.

Tracy, David. *The Analogical Imagination: Christian Theology and the Culture of Pluralism*. New York, 1981.

Vanderlaan, E. C. *Protestant Modernism in Holland*. Oxford, 1924.

Vidler, A. *The Language of the Gospel: Early Christian Rhetoric*. New York, 1964.

———. *Otherworldliness and the New Testament*. New York, 1954.

Index

The index contains items, especially names, not only from the text but also from the notes because many items in the notes do not refer directly to the text but provide important supplemental materials. There is no index to scriptural verses as such because the book was not constructed on that basis.